THE GOLDEN ANTHOLOGY

***

Writings of
John C. Papademetriou
A Greek-American Soldier in Korea
(1947-1951)

Compiled and Edited By
Dean Papademetriou

SOMERSET HALL PRESS
416 Commonwealth Avenue, Suite 117
Boston, Massachusetts 02215

© Copyright 2003 Constantine Papademetriou
Published by Somerset Hall Press
416 Commonwealth Avenue, Suite 117
Boston, Massachusetts 02215

All rights reserved. No part of this publication may be reproduced, stored in a retrieval system, or transmitted in any form or by any means- electronic, mechanical, photocopy, recording, or any other-without the prior written permission of the publisher. The only exception is brief quotations in printed reviews.

Library of Congress Control Number: 2003090234

CONTENTS

Acknowledgments   vii
Introduction, by Dean Papademetriou   ix

IN MEMORIAM

Obituary (Greek original)   3
Obituary (English Translation)   5

In Memoriam (Greek original), by Spyridon C. Papademetriou   7
In Memoriam (English Translation)   8
For John's Memory, by George C. Papademetriou   9
Memories of John, by Olga Marudas   10
Remembering My Brother John, by Evangelos C. Papademetriou   11
How I Remember My Brother John, by Alkiviades C. Papademetriou   13
Memories in Pictures   15

The Golden Anthology

JOHN'S STORY

John's Prologue: Knowledge   35
John's Story   37
Letters   51

ESSAYS

Life in Greece

The Senses   65

My Grandfather	66
What Happened to Me on July 15, 1938	67
Life in the Concentration Camp	68
The Conquerors and I	69

Life in America

Thanks to My New Country	72
The Streets of Moline (Illinois)	73
My Experience in a Grocery Store	74
The Moline Public Library	75
In Defense of Speaking One's Native Tongue	76
The Success of Greek Immigrants	77
Not the School, But the Students	79

John's Philosophy of Life

Great Power in Words	80
We All Love Life	81
Philosophy	82
Abraham Lincoln	83

Patriotism

Greek Heroism	84
Greece for Political and Territorial Independence	85
The Russian Bear	86
The Atomic Bomb	87

POEMS

Philosophy

Philosophy	91
God's Blessing	91
God	92
Red River	93
My Philosophy	94
You'll Be Happy to Live	94
On My Birthday	95

Patriotism

War Song	96
Ode to My Town, Karpenisi	96
Ode to the Greeks	97
War Song (II)	98
Greek and Italian War in Albania: A Little Drama	99
Europe	100
Hitler and Victory	101
To My Country	101
Hymn of Love	102
Glory	103
World War III	103

Korea

In Korea	105
Honor	106
Evening Prayer	107
My Foxhole	108
Easter in Korea	109
No!	110
Company "B"	111
I Shall Return	112

Love

My Advice	113
False Oath	115
To the Young Lady	115
Sweet Friend	116
Remember	117
The First Time I Saw You	118
Love	119
The Lamentation	119

POEMS IN GREEK

Greek originals	120

ACKNOWLEDGMENTS

In compiling and editing this volume of writings by my late uncle John C. Papademetriou, I received help from many people.

My father, Rev. George C. Papademetriou, my aunt Olga Marudas, and my uncles Rev. Spyridon, Evangelos, and Alkiviades Papademetriou, preserved their brother John's memory over the years. In particular, Evangelos safely kept most of John's original writings. As I started this project, they all contributed additional materials as well as their memories of John.

My father and my mother, Presvytera Athanasia Papademetriou, have provided tremendous encouragement and emotional and financial support throughout this project and all my life.

My brother Tom Papademetriou, a history professor, gave me numerous valuable suggestions on the best way to reveal John's story. My sister Jane P. Kourtis, John's namesake, has given me practical advice and support in many matters over the years.

Herald Gjura professionally laid out this book. But he went beyond the call of duty, and gave me the benefit of numerous publishing tips from his own experience.

Above all, I would like to thank my late uncle John for sacrificing his life to preserve American ideals, and for leaving us these writings as his legacy.

INTRODUCTION

Dean Papademetriou

My Uncle John was killed in action during the Korean War in 1951, before I was born. John's death had a huge impact on his whole family. John had many special qualities and he was so loved that his parents and siblings felt the loss intensely. Over ten years after John's death, two of John's brothers, my father George and my uncle Evangelos, even named their children, my sister Jane and my cousin John respectively, after John.

As I was growing up, my family would often visit John's grave at Arlington National Cemetery, outside of Washington, D.C., to conduct memorial services. Sometimes, my grandparents, aunts, uncles, and cousins would join us. As time went by, however, the bittersweet memory of John slowly receded for those family members who had known John personally: his brothers Spyridon, George, Evangelos, and Alkiviades, and his sister Olga. For the cousins in my generation who had never met him, John was a presence in family stories, but not a real person. The Korean War in which John was killed, and even the larger Cold War, ended. His siblings had children and grandchildren of their own. From Greek immigrants, they became fully integrated into American society. Life goes on.

What now makes John feel real to me is the fact that he was a prolific writer, something about him that I never knew before. For many years, John's brothers and sister treasured his writings, and kept them safe after his death. Nevertheless, no one had read them for a long time.

The fiftieth anniversary of John's death has renewed the family's interest in John's writings. John's writings finally make him feel real to me, and to others of my generation. After reading some of his writings, I finally have a clearer picture of what he was like as a Greek-American immigrant, as a soldier in the Korean war, and as a member of my family.

A Biographical Sketch

A sketch of John's short life comes from family souvenirs, oral history, and his own writings. John was born in Petralona, Greece on February 20, 1929. He was raised in the mainland mountain state of Evrytania, in the towns of Petralona and Hohlia, near the larger city of Karpenisi. His parents were the late Rev. Constantine Papademetriou and Presvytera Ourania (Katsifas) Papademetriou. He was the third of six children. His surviving siblings are Spyridon, Olga, George (my father), Evangelos, and Alkiviades.

As a child, John loved nature and the open air. Although he lived in a small town, he loved wandering alone in the countryside. On one occasion, he became lost and frightened, but luckily a young shepherd found him, and led him home. Touchingly, he cried with joy to see his mother and siblings again.

In 1939, when John was ten years old, his father, a Greek Orthodox priest, left Greece for the United States. Although John's father intended to send for the rest of the family as soon as he was settled, World War II broke out, and all travel was restricted. The family was to remain separated for almost ten years.

During the War, other relatives watched over the family. For a time, John lived with his father's father, George, in the nearby state of Thessaly. Pappou (grandfather) George had immigrated to the United States in the 1890's. He worked in railroad construction for several years. After he saved enough money, he returned to Greece, where he bought a general store, farmland, and many farm animals. Although he lived prosperously in Greece for the rest of his life, he told John stories about America, spurring John's imagination. Pappou George told John that, despite his hard work in the United States, he also managed to enjoy himself there.

The hardship and horror of the War soon reached John personally. In 1941, some Italian soldiers captured John as he was walking near his grandfather's house. He was held in a concentration camp for six months under terrible conditions. As he wrote later, there was little food, and even that was "not fit for chickens." He slept on the cement. Although he was the youngest boy in the camp, he was treated as harshly as the older men were.

During this time, John had a very close brush with death. The Italian guards of the concentration camp rounded up a large group of prisoners for execution. John was included in this group. Just as he was about to be executed, two German soldiers saw how young he was, and took pity on him. They took him out of the group to be executed, and saved him. The concentration camp finally released John after the Red Cross petitioned on his behalf.

After the War, in 1947, John and his family moved to the United States. They were finally reunited with their father. The family went to live in Moline, Illinois, where their father, Rev. Constantine, was a priest.

By then, John was eighteen years old. Because he knew no English, he enrolled at Calvin Coolidge Junior High School. With the encouragement of his teachers and librarians, he learned English, and quickly advanced to Moline High School. In high school, two teachers, Miss Hendee and Miss Johnson, took a special interest in him. With their encouragement, he started writing, which became his passion.

The Korean War

John graduated from Moline High School on June 9, 1950, just a few weeks before the North Korean army invaded South Korea on June 24, 1950. As John was deciding what to do after graduation, senior military and political officials were deciding what the United States response should be to the North Korean attack.

On July 23, 1950, John took a test for the U.S. Army, and enlisted the next day. At the same time, Army General Douglas MacArthur, the commander of the Army in Asia, recommended the commitment of American ground forces to defend South Korea from communist aggression. President Harry S. Truman approved this recommendation.

Military historians criticize the U.S. entry into the Korean War for several reasons. First, this was the first time that American soldiers were deployed to fight Asians on the Asian mainland. Second, the Americans underestimated the strength of the North Korean troops. Third, the U.S. intervened in the Korean civil war not for strategic interests in Asia, but to contain communism, and to teach Moscow a "lesson."

As the military drama unfolded, John was not aware of the high-level political discussions regarding the Korean War. Rather, John enlisted out of a sense of idealism. By February 1951, John had finished his training as an Army medical combat technician, and was stationed in Korea. He had the chance to stay on a military base in Japan, but he asked to be sent to the war zone. Other soldiers tried to warn John about the harsh conditions in Korea, but John never shirked what he saw as his duty to be on the front lines.

As an enlisted medic, John was qualified to give general first aid, to bandage wounds, and to give sedatives. Because of his dedication and skill, John was referred to as "Moline's Mountain Doctor" and as "Doc the Greek." In an interview after the War, another medic described his role as follows: "On the front lines, a doctor could have done little more than I. In any case, no one can complain that our forward aid station didn't give immediate service to the infantry." John would have faced a similar situation.

While the U.S. assisted South Korea, China assisted North Korea. During the first two weeks of May 1951, there was a build-up of Chinese troops. By May 10, an all-out Chinese offensive was imminent. In fact, there was heavy gun-fire during that entire period. This is when John showed his ultimate bravery, and paid with his life on May 12. His heroism was described on his posthumous Silver Star certificate:

> AWARD OF THE SILVER STAR — By direction of the President, under the provisions of the Act of Congress…, the Silver Star for gallantry in action is awarded posthumously to the following named enlisted man:

PRIVATE FIRST CLASS JOHN C. PAPADEMETRIOU, RA17282405, Army Medical Service, United States Army, a member of Medical Company, 9th Infantry Regiment, 2d Infantry Division, distinguished himself by gallantry in action on 12 May 1951 in the vicinity of Ankyon-ni, Korea. On that day, he was an aidman attached to a rifle company attacking well entrenched enemy forces on Hill 699. Private Papademetriou left his position of comparative safety on three separate occasions and braved the deadly enemy fire to administer first aid to wounded comrades. Upon hearing that a seriously wounded man had fallen in an exposed position, he immediately dashed to the soldier's side and started dressing his wounds. While attempting to move his comrade to safety, he was mortally wounded by a burst of enemy automatic weapons fire. Private Papademetriou's gallantry and devotion to his comrades reflect great credit upon himself and the military service. Entered the military service from Illinois.

BY COMMAND OF MAJOR GENERAL RUFFNER.

Unfortunately, John did not live to be part of the U.S. withdrawal from the Korean War. As casualties mounted, public support eroded for the war in Korea. By October 1951, a poll showed that 66% of the U.S. public thought that the war was "an utterly useless war." The mounting casualties, and the loss of public support, forced the U.S. to enter into peace negotiations. On November 27, 1951, the two sides agreed upon a truce line, which eventually became the final line, with minor adjustments.

Even after the truce line was determined, the fighting continued while the rest of the treaty was negotiated. Finally, two political events were pivotal in pushing along the negotiations. First, President Dwight D. Eisenhower was sworn into office in January 1953. Second, the U.S.S.R. leader Joseph Stalin died on March 15, 1953. With the resulting changes in leadership, an armistice was signed on July 27, 1953.

The Korean War, which was not declared as a war until recently, resulted in huge numbers of casualties. The Pentagon estimated that there were 2.4 million total military casualties. Of these, there were 54,246 American dead, and 103,284 American wounded. In addition, there were 2 million civilian casualties on both sides.

Without a clear-cut victory, both North and South Korea have remained in a state of tension for many years. The U.S. Army continues to maintain a military presence, and to support the South Korean regime. It is hoped that a lasting peace will someday come to this region.

John was buried on November 14, 1951 at Arlington National Cemetery. His entire family attended the funeral and burial. John's parents accepted John's posthumously awarded Silver Star and Purple Heart medals.

John's death left something missing in his family. Many years later, his mother, Ourania, analogized the loss of one of her children to losing a finger. John's wise mother always said that, although the other fingers remain, the hand still hurts.

John's Writing As An Expression Of His Idealism

As soon as John started learning English, he began writing. At the same time, his constant writing helped him practice his new language skills. His first essays were school assignments, but later he wrote on his own. It is remarkable that John's teachers took such a personal interest in him. They must have seen some promise in the young Greek immigrant, and they encouraged him to keep learning and writing.

The major theme that runs through John's writings is his idealism. This is expressed in several contexts, as will be discussed more fully below.

First, John wrote of his experience in Korea, where, out of a sense of duty, he volunteered for the front lines in the Korean Conflict. John enlisted in the Army just as the Korean Conflict was starting. He joined the medical corps as a way of helping others. Out of a sense of duty, he volunteered to go to the heart of the war zone in Korea.

Second, John wrote fondly of his life in Greece. As a sort of time capsule, his writings provide a glimpse of pre-War life in Greece, sometimes cozy, sometimes harsh. John idealized Greece, his beloved country of birth. In his essays, John tenderly described the people and things in his everyday life. For example, he wrote about his mother's cooking, his grandfather's musical talents, his school, and his love of nature, especially when he had the opportunity to lie under the clouds, alone, outside of town. He also described traumatic events, especially his hardships in a concentration camp, and his close brush with death. Despite this terrible experience, John defended Greece, insisting that "she did everything she could to protect" him. He was sensitive to charges that Greece was too weak to save her people during the War. In fact, he referred in many essays and poems to the glorious past of Greece, as well as to how Greece continued to live up to her heritage.

Third, other writings describe the hopeful and grateful life of immigrants in America's heartland, despite the difficulties. As an immigrant, John was very proud of his new home, the United States. He saw it as upholding and continuing the democratic ideals of Greece. His description of life in his new home is hopeful about the future. The stories of his beloved grandfather, who had enjoyed living in the United States many years before, must have remained in his imagination, and influenced his positive view of his new home. John admired the new places he saw, marveling at the buildings and clean streets.

At the same time, the life of an immigrant was not easy, and John applauded the intelligent and hard-working Greek immigrants. He wrote about the great accomplishments of Greeks throughout the world, and in America. Even with respect to uneducated immigrants, he insisted that they are the descendants of a noble race. His teachers, enlightened philhellenes themselves, encouraged this thinking. For example, in one essay, John wrote about the possibility of finding "a modern Phidias in a boot-black parlor." His teacher's comment about this possibility was as follows: "I found one, a fine student and cultured Greek, in a shoe shine parlor in Moline. This surprised me much. But this was before I knew Greeks."

His one criticism of the United States was of the prejudice and discrimination against immigrants. He must have been surprised by such attitudes towards Greeks, in particular, in light of his idealization of the glorious Greek past, as well as of his teachers' philhellenism. In a brave moment, he defended the immigrants' use of their native languages, arguing that everyone should be free to preserve their own traditions.

Fourth, his writings state his philosophy of life, and describe the people and ideas that inspired him. John's love for his two countries was part of his overall idealistic philosophy of life, which manifested itself in several ways. John's idealism included a belief in the great power of words to influence people. He tried to implement this belief through his own prolific writing. In addition, John recognized the importance of life. He was grateful that his own life was spared in the concentration camp, and that he was embarking on a new life in America. Furthermore, his heroes were the glorious heroes of Greece and the United States. For Greek heroes, he looked to the Golden Age of classical Greece to admire Pericles, who established democracy in Athens, and the great philosophers. His American heroes were George Washington and Abraham Lincoln. In particular, he admired Lincoln's development into a self-made man through his love of learning. He also respected Lincoln's opposition to slavery.

Fifth, another significant aspect of John's idealism is his intense patriotism. As stated above, John loved his two countries. This intense patriotism led to a glorification of dying for one's country. John's writings, especially his poems, worship the warrior ideal. He refers often to democracy, honor, and freedom. His writings were informed by his own World War II experiences. He saw his survival in the concentration camp as a specific example of the general bravery of Greeks in World War II.

Considering that John was writing at the beginning of the Cold War, his idealism and patriotism were, understandably, fiercely anti-communist. In contrast to his glorification of American and Greek warriors, he refers pejoratively to "Reds" and "the Russian bear." His anti-communist position is ironic in light of the huge personal impact on his life of the World War II fascists, who kept him in the concentration camp. His position is also interesting because he immigrated to the United States in 1947, during the vicious Greek civil war between communist and anti-communist partisans. Some of John's relatives were committed communists, including his father's brother, Seraphim, an intellectual who spent many years in jail for his communist political beliefs. Nevertheless, John's father, Rev. Constantine, was very conservative, even a royalist, and encouraged John's anti-communist stand.

John's glorification of heroic death for his country provides a strong contrast to his love of life. Yet, the glorification of heroic death comes out of the same idealism, the same hope for a better tomorrow. Especially in his poems, John encourages warriors not to think of their own lives, but only of their country. In his own experience in Korea, he insisted on going to the front lines out of patriotic duty, even though several fellow soldiers, and even his officers, tried to dissuade him. His expressed wish for patriotic death was unfortunately realized.

Sixth, John's idealism is also evident in his love poems. In theme, they are similar to Western European court poetry. The love object in the poems is never accessible, and always rejects him. In some cases, he takes revenge by forecasting the love object's lonely, loveless old age. In most cases, however, he himself is miserable about the rejection.

Finally, John was idealistic in his desire to see his writings published. He had a title for his book, *The Golden Anthology*, and sketched the cover design. John even found a publisher who accepted John's manuscript for publication. Edward Uhlan, the publisher of the Exposition Press in New York, wrote the following words of encouragement in a letter to John dated August 9, 1950:

> For someone who has not been born and raised in this country, you have managed remarkably well to assimilate yourself in the true American Spirit. I must commend you for a well-done job, for I think that you have, indeed, won! No one of intelligence can dismiss the long line of philosophy and free thinking that has been our inheritance from your ancestors of "the glory that was Greece." And to find that this long chain is still unbroken by

present-day writers is even more remarkable. Democracy is not a finely attenuated process, but one that has grown in substance and fiber; we have fought to keep a glorious inheritance alive, and it is pleasant to see one, such as you, still being inspired by the flame which came originally from your homeland. It would indeed be a tragedy if that flame were finally blown out, and through such books as the one you sent us, I feel that those who read your verse and prose will be instilled with much the same feeling that you yourself have towards this country and to your native land, which has now long suffered under alien oppression.

Unfortunately, John was killed in action before his writings could be published. Fifty years later, however, it is time to honor John's memory with the publication of his work. This volume collects the essays and poems that were part of his original *The Golden Anthology*, as well as some additional writings and letters. Although the writings have been edited and, in some cases, translated, they all contain John's essence. Publishing John's work is a testament to the idealism of a young man of another era.

Sources for Korean War Section

1. Clay Blair, *The Forgotten War – Americans in Korea 1950-1953*, New York: Anchor Books, Doubleday (1987).
2. John G. Westover, *Combat Support in Korea*, Washington, D.C.: Center of Military History, United States Army (1987). A collection of interviews with Korean Conflict armed forces members.

IN MEMORIAM

ΙΩΑΝΝΗΣ ΚΩΝΣΤΑΝΤΙΝΟΥ ΠΑΠΑΔΗΜΗΤΡΙΟΥ

[Ἀπό τήν Ἐφημερίδα Ἀτλαντίς]

Τήν Τετάρτην, 14ην Νοεμβρίου 1951, ἐτελέσθη εἰς τό Ἐθνικόν Νεκροταφεῖον τοῦ Arlington, Virginia, ἡ κηδεία τῆς σοροῦ τοῦ ἐν Κορέᾳ ἡρωικῶς πεσόντος ἀειμνήστου Ἰωάννου Κωνστ. Παπαδημητρίου τρίτο κου υἱοῦ τοῦ ἱερέως Κωνστ. Παπαδημητρίου ἐφημερίου τῆς Ἑλληνορθοδόξου Κοινότητος τοῦ Ἁγίου Γεωργίου ἐν Moline, Illinois. Τήν νεκρώσιμον ἀκολουθίαν ἔψαλλεν ὁ Αἰδεσ. Εὐστρ. Σπυρόπουλος, προσκληθείς πρός τοῦτο ὑπό τῆς ἁρμοδίας Στρατιωτικῆς ἀρχῆς, καί ὁ πατήρ τοῦ μεταστάντος, εἰς τό παρεκκλήσιον τοῦ Νεκροταφείου. Κατ' αὐτήν παρευρέθησαν οἱ γονεῖς, οἱ ἀδελφοί του Αἰδεσ. Σπυρίδων Παπαδημητρίου μετά τῆς πρεσβυτέρας του, Γεώργιος, Εὐάγγελος καί Ἀλκιβιάδης Παπαδημητρίου, κ. Σταῦρος Μαρούδας σύζυγος τῆς Ὄλγας, ἀδελφῆς τοῦ ἀειμνήστου, ἐκ Νέας Ὑόρκης, ὁ θεῖος του κ. Γεώργιος Κλειτσάκης μετά τῆς ἀξιοτίμου κυρίας Δημητρίου καί τῆς ἀδελφῆς τῆς ἐκ Wilmington, Delaware ὁ θεῖος του κ. Γεώργιος Τσούνης ἐκ Charleston, West Virginia, καί ἄλλοι.

Μετά τό πέρας τῆς νεκρωσίμου ἀκολουθίας Στρατιωτική ὁμάς συνώδευσε τό φέρετρον μέχρι τοῦ τάφου, ὅπου μετά τήν τελετήν τοῦ τρισαγίου παρεδόθη εἰς τήν μητέρα τοῦ ἥρωος Πρεσβυτέραν Οὐρανίαν Παπαδημητρίου ἡ ἀστερρόεσσα τήν ὁποίαν ὁ ἀείμνηστος ἐτίμησε διά τῆς αὐτοθυσίας του. Ἐκεῖθεν ἅπαντες μετέβησαν ἐπί ἕξ αὐτοκινήτων διατεθέντων ὑπό τοῦ Ἐρυθροῦ Σταυροῦ εἰς τό Γραφεῖον τοῦ Νεκροταφείου ὅπου ἀφοῦ ἐδέχθησαν τά συλλυπητήρια τοῦ Διευθυντοῦ τοῦ Νεκροταφείου παρέλαβεν αὐτούς ἀξιωματικός τοῦ Γραφείου τούτου καί συνώδευσε μέχρι τοῦ Πενταγώνου (Pentagon) Δημοσίου κτηρίου ὅπου στεγάζεται ἡ ὑπηρεσία τῶν στρατιωτικῶν ὅπου καί ἐμίλησαν περί τοῦ ἡρωικοῦ θανάτου τοῦ ἀειμνήστου, προσπαθήσαντος νά σώση τραματίας συναδέλφους του ἐν ὥρᾳ μάχης. Μετ' αὐτό ἐνώπιον εἰκοσάδος ἀνωτέρων καί κατωτέρων ἀξιωματικῶν ὡμίλησεν ὁ στρατηγός κ. W.E. Bergin, Major General USA ἐξάρας τήν αὐτοθυσίαν, τήν φιλοπατρίαν καί τάς ἄλλας ἀρετάς τάς ὁποίας εἶχεν ὡς στρατιώτης ὁ μεταστάς καί ἐπέδωκεν εἰς τόν πατέρα τοῦ ἥρωος Αἰδεσ. Κωνστ. Παπαδημητρίου Μετάλιον τοῦ Silver Star διά τήν ἐξαιρετικήν ὑπηρεσίαν ἥν προσέφερεν ὁ υἱός του ἐξ ὀνόματος τοῦ Προέδρου τῶν Η.Π.Α. καί τοῦ Ὑπουργοῦ τῶν Στρατιωτικῶν, ἀναγνώσας καί τό σχετικόν ἔγγραφον. Ἔπειτα ἀνεχώρησαν ἅπαντες βαθύτατα συγκεκινημένοι.

Ὁ ἀείμνηστος Ἰωάννης ἐγενήθη εἰς τά Πετράλωνα τῆς Εὐρυτανίας τήν 20ην Φεβρουαρίου 1929. Ἐφοίτησεν εἰς τό Δημοτικόν Σχολεῖον τῆς πατρίδος του ἀλλά λόγω τῆς ἐπελθούσης Γερμανοϊταλικῆς κατοχῆς καί τῶν μετέπειτα γεγονότων δέν ἠδυνήθη νά ἐξακολουθήσει. Τό 1947, 5 Φεβρουαρίου ἀπεβιβάσθη εἰς Νέαν Ὑόρκην μετά τῆς μητρός του καί τῶν ἄλλων ἀδελφῶν του καί ἦλθε εἰς Moline, Illinois τήν 7ην Φεβρουαρίου, ὅπου καί ἐνεγράφη ἀμέσως εἰς τήν 8ην τάξιν τοῦ Calvin Coolidge Jr. High School ἀπεφοίτησε μετά τιμῶν καί ἐπαίνων ἀπό τό High School τόν Ἰούνιον 1950. Ἐκεῖ ἦτο ἀγαπητός εἰς ὅλους, διδάσκοντας καί διδασκόμενους διά τήν φιλομάθειαν του καί ἐργατικότητά του.

Ἕνα καί ἥμισυ μῆνα ἀργότερα μέ ὑπηρηφάνειαν κατετάχθη εἰς τόν Ἀμερικανικόν Στρατόν. Τήν 25ην Ἰουλίου 1950 ἔδωκεν εἰς Des Moines, Iowa τόν νενομισμένον ὅρκον καί ἀμέσως ἔγραψεν εἰς τούς γονεῖς του ὅτι: "Σήμερον ὡρκίσθην ὅτι θά ὑπηρετήσω πιστῶς τήν Σημαία τῶν ΗΠΑ καί θά τό κάμω" καί τό ἔκαμε. Ἐκεῖθεν μετέβη εἰς τό Ford Ord, California, ἀφ' ὅπου ἀπεσπάσθη εἰς τό Medical Service, San Antonio, Texas, ὅπου ἐξαιπεδεύθη ὡς στρατιωτικός Νοσοκόμος καί τήν 3ην Ἰανουαρίου 1951 μετεφέρθη μέ 15θήμερον ἄδειαν εἰς τούς γονεῖς του καί τήν 19ην τοῦ ἰδίου ἀνεχώρησεν διά Καλιφόρνιαν προοριζόμενος διά Κορέαν. Πρό τῆς ἀναχωρήσεώς του μετέβη καί ἐκκλησιάσθη διά τελευταίαν φοράν εἰς τήν Ἑλληνικήν Ὀρθόδοξον Ἐκκλησία τοῦ Ἁγίου Φραγκίσκου καί ἔγραψεν ἀμέσως εἰς τόν πατέρα του: "Σήμερα ἐπῆγα εἰς τήν ἐκκλησίαν γιατί αὔριον ἀναχωρῶ διά τήν Ἰαπωνίαν. Εἶμαι περήφανος διότι κατάγομαι ἀπό Ἕλληνας γονεῖς καί Ἱερατικήν τάξιν. Εἶμαι ὑπερήφανος διότι γεννήθηκα εἰς τήν χώραν τῆς Δόξης πού λέγεται Ἑλλάς. Εἶμαι ὑπερήφανος γιατί ἀνήκω εἰς τήν ἀληθινήν ἐκκλησίαν τοῦ Χριστοῦ τήν Ὀρθόδοξον.

Ἤκουσα ὡραῖα λόγια διά τήν Ἐκκλησίαν μας ἀπό τόν ἱερέα τῆς Νέας Γενεᾶς. Σέ παρακαλῶ νά μέ γράψεις χωριστά ἀπό τήν οἰκογένεια διά τό Δεκαδολλάριον καί μοῦ στείλης τήν κάρτα μου". Ἔγραφε καθημερινῶς εἰς τούς γονεῖς του καί τά ἀδέλφια του μέχρι τῆς ἡμέρας καθ' ἥν Θεία θελήσει ἔφυγεν ἀπό τήν ζωήν αὐτήν.

Τήν 12ην Μαΐου 1951 μετέβη εἰς τήν ὑπηρεσίαν του καί καθ' ἥν ὥραν εὐσυνειδήτως ἐξετέλει ταύτην, ἄσπλαχνος ἐχθρική σφαῖρα τόν ἄφηκεν νεκρόν, χωρίς νά λυπηθῆ τά εἰκοσιένα του χρόνια. Τήν 27ην Μαΐου τό Ὑπουργεῖον τῶν Στρατιωτικῶν εἰδοποίησε τούς γονεῖς του.

Ὁ ἀείμνηστος εὑρισκόμενος εἰς τήν Ἑλλάδα τό 1941, ἐκρατήθη ἐπί ἕξ μῆνες καί πλέον θεωρηθείς ὡς ἐξασφανισθείς εἰς τό στρατόπεδον συγκεντρώσεως Λαρίσσης ὑπό τῶν Γερμανοϊταλῶν.

Εἴθε ὁ Πανάγαθος Θεός νά κατατάξη τήν ἀθώαν του ψυχήν μετά τῶν Ἁγίων καί νά στείλη βάλσαμον παρηγορίας εἰς τούς ἀπαρηγόρητους γονεῖς, ἀδελφούς καί λοιπούς συγγενεῖς του.

JOHN CONSTANTINE PAPADEMETRIOU

[Editor's Note: This obituary was originally published in Greek (printed above) in the Greek-American newspaper, *Atlantis*.]

On Wednesday, November 14, 1951, the funeral of the Korean War hero John C. Papademetriou took place at the National Cemetery in Arlington, Virginia. John was the third child of the Rev. Constantine Papademetriou from the Greek Orthodox community of St. George in Moline, Illinois. The funeral service was chanted by the Rev. Eustratios Spyropoulos, who was invited by military officials to perform this service, and by John's father. The funeral service was held at the chapel of the National Cemetery.

At the funeral, John's parents were present, as well as his brothers, Rev. Spyridon Papademetriou, George, Evangelos, and Alkiviades. Also present were his sister Olga's husband, Steve Marudas, from New York; his uncle, George Klitsakis, accompanied by Mrs. Demetriou and her sister, from Wilmington, Delaware; his uncle, George Tsiounis, from Charleston, West Virginia; and others.

Following the funeral service, the military procession accompanied the bier to the grave. After the trisagion memorial service, the ceremonial American flag was given to the hero's mother, Presvytera Ourania Papademetriou. It was the American flag that John so greatly honored, and for which he offered himself for its glory.

Following that ceremony, the Red Cross transported the family to the Pentagon, where officials spoke of John's heroic sacrifice while tending to the wounded in battle. Following the many speeches by Army officers, Major General W. E. Bergin, U.S.A., spoke praising John's self-sacrifice and love for his country. The general gave to John's father, the Rev. Constantine Papademetriou, on behalf of the President of the U.S.A. and the Secretary of the Army, the Silver Star medallion, and read the pertinent text. After that, everyone departed deeply moved with sorrow.

The late John Papademetriou was born in Petralona, Evrytania, on February 20, 1929. He attended the elementary school in his native land, but did not continue his schooling during the occupation of Greece by the Germans. On February 5, 1947, he came to New York with his mother and siblings. He arrived in Moline, Illinois on February 7, 1947, where he registered in the 8th grade at Calvin Coolidge Junior High

School. He graduated with honors from Moline High School in June 1950. At high school, he was greatly loved by teachers and students for his love of learning and hard work.

A month and a half later, he entered the American Army. On July 25, 1950, he was sworn in, at Des Moines, Iowa. He wrote to his parents immediately: "Today, I took the oath of office that I will serve faithfully the U.S. flag, and I will do it." He did exactly that. Afterwards, he was sent to Fort Ord, California, and was assigned to the medical corps. In San Antonio, Texas, he was trained at the military hospital, and then he had two weeks furlough, during which he visited his parents. On January 19, 1951, he left for California, and from there went to Korea.

Before leaving for Korea, he attended for the last time the Greek Orthodox Church service in San Francisco. He wrote to this father: "Today, I went to church because tomorrow I depart for Japan. I am proud because I serve the glorious American flag. I am proud to be a descendant of Greek parents and a priestly family. I am proud to have been born in the glorious land that is called Greece. I am proud to belong to the true church of Christ, the Orthodox Church.

"I heard beautiful words about our Church from the young American-bred priest. I would like to request you please to enroll me, separately from the family, into Church membership and pay my dues, and send my membership card." He wrote daily to his parents, and to his brothers and sister, until the day he was taken from this life by the Divine Will.

On May 12, 1951, as he was serving with great devotion the needs of his fellow soldiers – the wounded – an enemy bullet, without compassion for his youth, left him dead at the young age of 21. On May 27, 1951, the Secretary of the Army informed his family.

The late John Papademetriou was detained during the War in 1941 at the German military center at Larissa for over 6 months, and he was considered disappeared.

May the Great, Good God place his innocent soul with the Saints, and bestow comfort on his inconsolable parents, brothers, sister, and all his relatives.

In Memoriam

ΑΘΑΝΑΤΟΙ ΝΕΚΡΟΙ ΔΕΚΑΝΕΥΣ ΙΩΑΝΝΗΣ Κ. ΠΑΠΑΔΗΜΗΤΡΙΟΥ

Αἰδ. Σπυρίδων Παπαδημητρίου

Ἦλθε πολλές φορές ὁ ταχυδρόμος σπίτι μας. Ἦλθε καί ἔφερνε ἀγγέλματα χαρᾶς, μηνύματα γάμων καί εὐχῶν. Ἦλθε ὅμως καί τήν παρελθοῦσαν Κυριακήν τό μεσημέρι. Μά ἀντί ἀγγέλματος χαρᾶς ἔφερε ἄγγελμα θλιβερό, ἀντί μηνύματος γάμων ἔφερε μήνυμα παρακαίρου θανάτου καί ἀντί εὐχῶν ἔφερε πικρό μοιρολόγι. Ἦλθε καί τό μήνυμα πούφερε, ἔλεγε: "Ὁ Γιάννης δέν ὑπάρχει πιά στή ζωή. Ἔπεσε τιμημένα στά 12 Μαΐου σέ κάποιο βουνό δόξης στήν Κορέα". Ὁ Γιάννης Παπαδημητρίου ἀπ' τά Πετράλωνα-Εὐρυτανίας λατρευτός υἱός τοῦ ἐν Moline, Illinois, ἱερέως Κων. Παπαδημητρίου καί τῆς πρεσβυτέρας του Οὐρανίας. Ἦλθε πρό τριῶν χρόνων μαζί μέ τήν μητέρα του καί πέντε ἀδέλφια του. Ἡ δραστηριότης του, ἡ φιλομάθειά του καί ἡ φιλοπονία του ἦσαν τά χαρίσματα ἐκεῖνα διά τά ὁποῖα ἠγαπᾶτο καί ἐθαυμάζετο ὄχι μόνον ἀπό τούς οἰκείους του, ἀλλά καί ἀπό ὅλους ὅσους τόν ἐγνώριζαν, καθηγητάς, συμφοιτητάς καί συνεργάτας του.

Ἐντός τριῶν χρόνων καί μέ ἀφάνταστη ὑπομονή καί ἐπιμονή ἐπέτυχε νά ἀποφοιτήσει μετά πολλῶν ἐπαίνων καί διακρίσεων τοῦ Ἀμερικανικοῦ Γυμνασίου. Καί ἀμέσως κατετάγη ἐθελοντής ὑπό τήν Ἀστερόεσσαν. Ἐξεπαιδεύθη εἰς τήν Καλιφόρνιαν καί κατόπιν κατηρτίσθη ὡς στρατιωτικός νοσοκόμος εἰς τό Τέξας.

Ὡς τοιοῦτος ἀνεχώρησε τήν 22αν Φεβρουαρίου διά τό μέτωπον τῆς Κορέας. Ἐκεῖ δέ πολλάκις ἐχρησίμευσε καί ὡς διερμηνεύς μεταξύ Ἑλλήνων καί Ἀμερικανῶν. Ἐκεῖνο ὅμως πού πρέπει νά σημειωθῆ ἰδιαιτέρως καί πού ἀφήνει ἀπαρηγορήτους τούς προσφιλεῖς του ἦτο ἡ μεγάλη του καρδιά καί ὁ χρυσός του χαρακτήρας.

Χαρακτηριστικό εἶναι ἕνα γράμμα του στήν Ἀρχιεπισκοπή, δημοσιευθέν καί στήν Ἀτλαντίδα, ζητῶντας νά βοηθήσῃ ἐκ τοῦ ὑστερήματός του ὀρφανά τῆς πατρίδος. Στό προτελευταῖο γράμμα του μούγραφε: "Ἐγώ δέν εἶμαι σπάταλος, γιατί τά χρήματα τῶν περιττῶν ἐξόδων μου καί νά μήν τά διαθέσω γιά ὀρφανά; Θυμοῦμαι καί ἐγώ στήν Ἑλλάδα, ἀποκλεισμένοι ἀπό τόν πατέρα μου λόγω τοῦ πολέμου, ἤμουνα σάν ὀρφανός ἀπ' ὅλους καταφρονεμένος". Μοὔστειλε ἀπ' τήν Κορέα, σάν ἀπομνημονεύματα, τήν ὅλην ὡς τότε δράσιν του. Διαβάζοντας κανείς αὐτό θαυμάζει μέ πόσην χαράν καί ὑπερηφάνειαν ὑπηρέτει ὑπό τήν Ἀστερόεσσαν.

Αἱ πολλές σου χάρες καί λεβεντιές, ἀγαπημένε μας Γιάννη, θά μένουν γιά μας διαρκές μνημόσυνον. Πάντα θά ψάλλουν σάν μυρωμένα λουλούδια τοῦ Μαγιοῦ πού μιά καταιγίδα του σέ μάρανε παράκαιρα. Ἔπεσες γιά τήν παγκόσμιο δικαιοσύνη καί σύ ὅπως καί τόσοι ἄλλοι πρόγονοί σου ἀγωνισταί τῶν Θερμοπυλῶν, τῆς Πίνδου καί τοῦ Γράμμου. Αἱ πατρίδες σου Ἑλλάδα καί Ἀμερική, ἅς σέ στεφανώσουν. Αἰωνία σου ἡ μνήμη.

IN MEMORIAM: IMMORTAL DEAD, CORPORAL JOHN C. PAPADEMETRIOU (U.S. ARMY MEDICAL CORPS)

Spyridon C. Papademetriou

[Editor's Note: This was originally published in Greek (printed above) in June 1951 in the New York Greek daily, *Atlantis*.]

Many a time the postman came to our house. He came bringing messages of joy; messages of weddings and glad tidings. He came also last Sunday at noontime; but instead of a joyful message, he brought us an announcement of grief. Instead of an announcement of a joyful event, he brought us a lamentation. He came and the message of a few words said: "John is not alive anymore; he fell with honor on May 12th at a hill of glory in Korea."

John Papademetriou was born in Petralona, Evrytania, beloved son of the Reverend Constantine and Presvytera Ourania Papademetriou of Moline, Illinois. He arrived from Greece three years ago, with his mother and his four brothers and sister. His efficiency, his diligence, his willingness to learn, and his charisma made him loved and admired not only by his family, but also by everyone who knew him: teachers, fellow students, and co-workers. With great effort and perseverance, he succeeded in graduating with honors from an American high school within three years of coming to America. Soon thereafter, he volunteered to serve in the Armed Services under the American flag. He had his basic training in California; and specialized in the medical corps in Texas. He left for the front lines of Korea on February 22, 1951. There, he also served as an interpreter between the Greek and American forces.

That which is to be noted most especially, and which leaves his beloved family inconsolable, was his good and passionate heart and his golden character.

Prior to his death, in a letter to the Greek Orthodox Archdiocese in New York, published also in New York's Greek daily *Atlantis*, he asked how to help the orphanage from his meager stipend he received as a soldier. "I'm not wasteful in my everyday life, why not use some of my stipend for the orphans? I remember when I was in Greece, without being able, because of the War, to communicate with father, I felt like an orphan disdained by everyone."

John was very prompt with his communications with his parents and family. He wrote of his life and experiences in the front lines, the far-away Korea. His writings reflect the pride and joy to serve under the Star Spangled Banner.

Dearly beloved John, your many charismas, bravery, and youthful vigor will always remain as a continuous memorial. They will always bloom as sweet May flowers, which a storm has cut off untimely. You gave your life for world justice and honor, as did so many others of your ancestors, at Thermopylae, in Marathon, and in Pindos during the Second World War. Both your countries (*patrides*), Greece and the United States of America, shall crown you.

+ May your memory be eternal.

FOR JOHN'S MEMORY

George C. Papademetriou

[Editor's Note: this was originally published in Spring 1952 in the Moline High School literary magazine, *The Imp.*]

Introduction: This is the memorial written by George Papademetriou to honor his brother, a young boy who came from Greece just a few years ago, who graduated from Moline high school, and who gave his life in the Korean campaign for the peace for which both Greece and America are searching.

I went to Washington for my brother John's funeral. My heart was beating hard and my feet were shaking. My mother had fainted, but my brother, Rev. Spyridon, had some medicine that revived her. Everybody was crying for John. Tears were coming down from our eyes. My mother was trying to get hold of the closed casket. She was calling aloud to John and pulling out of my brother's arms. He let her feel the casket and see that she couldn't touch John or see him any more. She was frenzied with grief, and she could not see anything. My father took little part in the funeral, for his heart also could not stand to part with his beloved son. My oldest brother (he is a priest in Massachusetts) couldn't stand to help with the funeral of his brother. He was crying like the rest of us. Tears were coming from my brother-in-law's eyes, but he was staying firm and saying to us that John had died for us. But nothing helped us at that time. We felt so bad that we did not care for ourselves. The time came, and my beloved brother was buried while we were crying and shaking. The rifles were fired and John's casket was lowered into the ground. He was laid to rest with thousands of his brothers in Arlington National Cemetery. My father received the Silver Star and the Purple Heart for John's heroism. I never before felt as bad in my life. I think that the end of my brother's life was the end of my mother's happiness in life.

MEMORIES OF JOHN

Olga Marudas

More than 50 years have passed since my brother John was "killed in action" in Korea. My memories of him are sometimes happy, and sometimes sad. Happy because we left a war in Greece unharmed, but sad because we arrived in America at the start of another war that took John's life. This was especially difficult for our Mother Ourania, who thought that we would all be safe here.

I have many memories of John, but two stand out. First, there was a time, while we were still in Greece and John was very young, that he became very sick. He was thus put on a strict diet, which was very hard on him and the whole family. He had to be watched carefully and constantly. On Easter Sunday, he could not eat what the rest of us were eating, so he took a whole loaf of *tsoureki* (sweet Easter bread), and hid from all of us so that he could eat it without being seen. The whole town went out to look for him. When we found him, he had of course eaten the whole loaf. All of us kids were blamed for not watching him.

The second memory that stands out is, when we arrived in America, John was the first one in the family to learn an American word. During the first two weeks here, John kept hearing everyone on crowded buses saying "sorry" as they pushed and shoved each other. John had an idea of what this word meant, but he wanted to find out for sure. He purposely stepped on someone's foot, and said "sorry." It was then that he knew he had learned an American word.

REMEMBERING MY BROTHER JOHN

Evangelos C. Papademetriou

Not many days go by when I don't remember my brother John since his death in 1951. My wife Loukia and I named our son after him.

I remember my brother John when we were children in Greece during World War II, especially in 1941 when he went to visit our paternal grandparents. There, he was captured by the Germans and the Italians, and was held for several months. When he was released and came home, he was white as a sheet from malnutrition, and hard of hearing in one ear. His ear was damaged when an interrogator slapped John on the side of the head because John would not answer the interrogator's questions.

I remember our family's trip to the United States of America in 1947. We boarded the ship Saturnia at the port of Piraeus, and went straight to the cabin. When we saw the bunk beds, John and I took the top beds, and made our brothers George and Alkiviades take the bottom beds. But in the middle of the Atlantic Ocean, when we got seasick, we took over the bottom beds.

I remember John when we came to the United States. We started school in Moline, Illinois, and John worked very hard. John did not like school that much in his early grades, and because of the war he only completed the fifth or sixth grade in Greece. Even though none of us spoke a word of English when we arrived in the United States, John managed to graduate from high school in three and a half years. In that time, we hardly saw John except on Sundays. John's daily routine was as follows: after breakfast, he went to school; after school, he would come home to have something to eat, and then he would leave for the public library or for work. He would not return home until late at night. His transportation was by bus or walking.

One of the funniest things I remember about John was that he never liked to eat squash or pumpkin of any kind, no matter how it was cooked. One day, he came home from school and went up to his room. As he was leaving, he stopped by the kitchen where our mother was cooking. She had just peeled and sliced some green squash, and it was ready to cook. Mother asked John to sit down to have something to eat and talk. John replied that he was in a hurry and did not have time, that he was going to the library, and that he would eat when he came home. With that, he grabbed a slice of squash, commented on how good the "cucumber" looked, started eating it, and ran out the kitchen door. Mother yelled after him, "Son, you don't eat squash when it's cooked, but you eat it raw?" In his haste, John did not hear her. Afterwards, when we told him that he had eaten squash and we made fun of him, John insisted that it was cucumber.

John liked to go to church, and was an altar boy. He helped in the Sanctuary in our village of Hohlia, Greece, and with the blessing of houses on certain holidays. He liked to dance and have fun. He was in the middle of every dance at weddings, holiday celebrations, and festivals. I remember having fun with my brother John. As children, we were always playing, dancing, singing, telling stories, arguing, and even fighting at times.

I remember when John joined the Army, and when he came home on leave after basic training, proudly wearing his uniform. When his leave was over, we walked him to the train station, the whole family. There, we embraced and kissed each other, and said our farewells. We waved as the train pulled out of the station, not knowing that we would be seeing each other for the last time. We feared that he would be going to Korea since the war had already started there. We did not discuss it much when he was home.

I remember Memorial Day, 1951, when our father gave us the awful news that John had been killed in action in the war in Korea. A few months later, we went to Washington D.C. for his military funeral at Arlington National Cemetery. I remember it was a gloomy, rainy day when we arrived by train at Union Station in Washington. We waited at the station for our whole family to arrive from Illinois and New York, and even our uncles George Tsiounis from West Virginia and George Klitsakis from Delaware. Only my sister Olga did not come because she had just had her baby daughter Nikki.

United States Army staff cars were waiting, and took us to the chapel at Arlington National Cemetery. There, we saw John's sealed casket for the first time. Our father, who was a Greek Orthodox priest, and the local Greek Orthodox priest read a small prayer. Then the Military Honor Guard draped the casket with the American flag and loaded it in a hearse instead of on a caisson because it was raining. We all followed the hearse in a procession to the burial site. The burial ceremony took place in the rain. The Honor Guard fired three volleys into the air, the bugler sounded taps, and the flag was folded and presented to our mother.

After the burial ceremony, we were taken to the Pentagon. At the Pentagon, the Army Chief of Staff General White presented our parents with the decorations that were awarded to John posthumously. He received the Silver Star for gallantry in action, and the Purple Heart for wounds received in the line of duty. We all felt great sorrow and great pride. (I still have the same feeling now when I visit Arlington National Cemetery and Washington, D.C.) After the ceremony at the Pentagon, we went to a Greek restaurant for the memorial dinner, and then we departed from Washington, D.C.

HOW I REMEMBER MY BROTHER JOHN

Alkiviades C. Papademetriou

I remember my brother John, back in 1951 when I was 15 years old, as a quiet and gentle person who was always busy with his schoolwork. In addition to his schoolwork, he worked hard daily to help himself financially. Each day after school, John traveled by bus to work and home.

John was well liked by those he worked with, as well as by his teachers and fellow students at school. In particular, he was very much liked by his English teacher who helped him write poetry that he loved so much.

When John was available, he would always offer his help to me with my schoolwork and never ceased giving me advice, as an older brother, on what he thought was very important for me.

As a much younger brother, I cannot remember everything about my brother, but there are always those few things you never forget. The first was when he took me to his company picnic and we shared in all the fun together. Unfortunately, I can also remember the time when he informed our family that he was going to join the United States Army.

We all tried our best to talk him out of it, but to no avail.

After joining the Army and spending some time there, he made some close friends. These three close friends would visit our family frequently just to say hello.

After some time, the day arrived for him to leave for the Korean War. This really hurt the family, especially my parents. Following his departure, we heard from him again a few months later, by mail, informing us that everything was going fine and that soon he would come visit us after his basic training. Sure enough, he came and visited us for two weeks and told us about the training he was receiving.

After spending two weeks with our family, it was time for him to leave again and return to his duties. The pain to see him leave again had returned to all of us. Little did we know that this was the last time we would see him alive!

While he was away, he communicated with us by mail. He sent us letters and pictures of himself and his friends overseas. As the time grew near for him to return home, he communicated with us more infrequently, but we all knew it would be quite soon when he would return so we waited with anticipation. Unfortunately, that day never came.

One bright afternoon in May, while I was home ill from school, a car arrived in front of our house. Two soldiers exited the car and approached our door. They rang the doorbell and I answered the door. They informed me that they had a telegram for us but would not give it to me because I was the only one home at the time. They said they would return later to give it to my father.

When they returned, my father was home to receive the telegram. After receiving the telegram, he proceeded to open it, and I immediately saw an expression on his face that told me something was wrong. When I asked him to tell me what it said, he would not. Then, I realized it had to be very sad news. I did not give much thought to the letter initially because I did not want to believe the worst was true.

Memorial Day came, and as we (my parents, my brother George, and I) sat down around the table to eat dinner, the time came for my father to break the news to us that John would not return home because he had been killed in Korea on that bright day in May. That bright day turned out to be the darkest day in our family's lives.

May God Rest John's Soul.

MEMORIES IN PICTURES

John's Grandparents in Greece. Clockwise from top left: Georgios Papademetriou; Paraskevi (Tsiringas) Papademetriou; Georgia (Tsiounis) Katsifas; and Konstantinos Katsifas.

Papademetriou Family Journey to America (1946-1947).
Top: Stop in Lamia, Greece.
Bottom: Arrival in America. Left to right: George, John, Evangelos, their mother Ourania, Alkiviades, their father Rev. Constantine, and Olga. (Spyridon in inset.)

John's Graduation from Moline (Illinois) High School, June 9, 1950.

At sister Olga's wedding to Steve Marudas, January 15, 1950.

In the Army for Basic Training. Fort Ord, Monterey, California, September 1950.

More Basic Training.

Medic Training. Brooke Hospital Center Headquarters, Brooke General Hospital, Fort Sam Houston, San Antonio Texas, October 1950.

Family Reunion in Moline, Illinois during John's leave, January 1951. Top left picture, left to right: (top row) George, John, and Evangelos; (bottom row) their mother Ourania, Alkiviades, and Rev. Constantine.

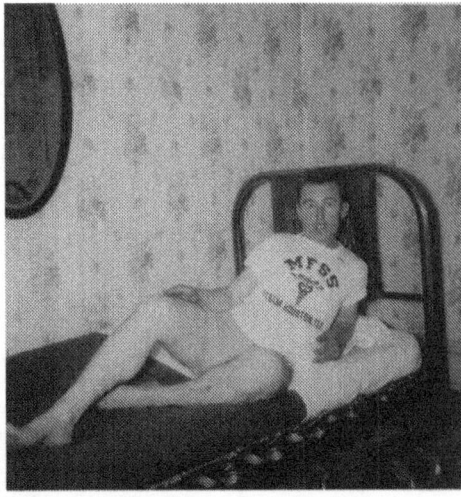

Crossing the Pacific aboard U.S.N.S. Howze, February 1951.

In the Army.

John's father Rev. Constantine receiving John's posthumous Purple Heart award (Alkiviades looking on).

John's parents, Rev. Constantine and Ourania, at John's gravesite at Arlington National Cemetery, Arlington, Virginia (outside Washington, D.C.).

John's Purple Heart and Silver Star certificates.

Family Visits to John's Gravesite.
Top left picture: The editor's family in 1969. Rev. George, Athanasia, Jane (John's namesake), Tom, and Dean. Top right picture: The editor's family with the Marudas family in 1971. John's sister Olga, her husband Steve Marudas, Jane, Candi Marudas, Dean, Tom, and Rev. George.

Papademetriou Family Reunion. Gathered at John's gravesite at Arlington National Cemetery, May 12, 2001 (exactly 50 years after John's death).

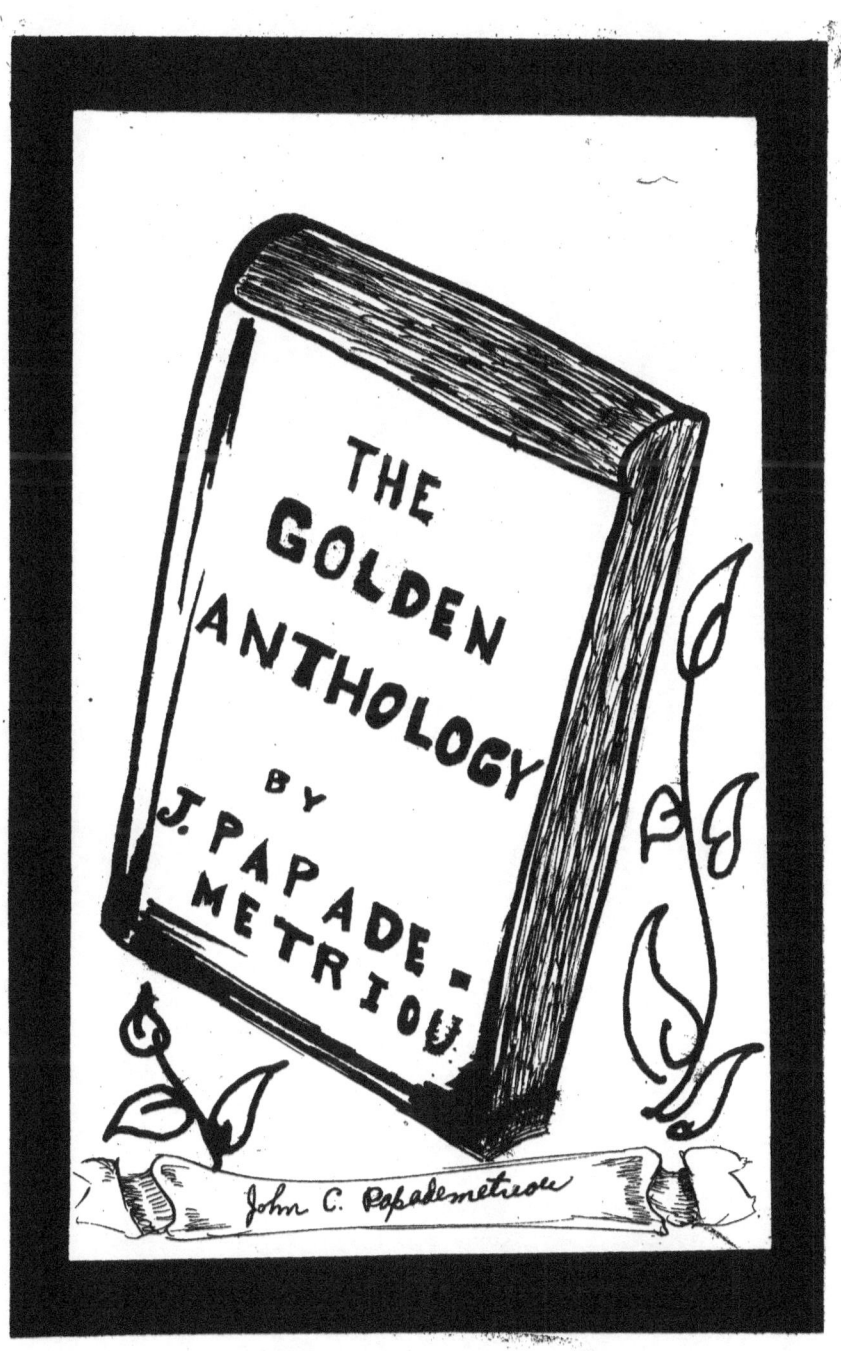

John's proposed cover for his book

The Golden Anthology

John C. Papademetriou

"Πάντων κτημάτων κράτιστον
εἴη φίλος σαφής καί ἀγαθός"

"The greatest of all possessions
is a sure and good friend"

JOHN'S STORY

JOHN'S PROLOGUE: KNOWLEDGE

I deeply appreciate this opportunity that I have had of coming over to America, and attending the United States public schools, which I love.

I remember my immigration day, the first day I came to America, February 5, 1947, when I couldn't speak English at all. I came over to this country without any experience of American life, without English speaking knowledge. I struggled with everything, but I won!

I must thank my teachers who had interest enough in me to help me, and also my fellow students, from whom I learned what I know today.

The poems I have been writing, I wrote with hard work. Every day after school, with my old Greek-English dictionary, I gained knowledge at the Moline Public Library, for almost one half year. The poems are my observations of my country, Greece, during my four years of life there during the War in 1941-1945. During World War II, my country suffered terribly, but I won't discuss it in this volume. The next volume will be composed of short stories and short poems.

[Editor's note: All writings have been combined in the present book.]

I would deeply appreciate giving an idea of my observations, during the two years I have been in America, about the Greeks in this country.

We, the Greeks who are assembled in this country of the United States of America, today are loyal friends of Democracy. We are bound together by common interests and ties. These include: love for the United States of America and Greece; admiration of Greek culture, talent, and courage; a desire to promote friendly relations in the united world of today; and determination to do all that is possible and proper to aid Greece to maintain her independence and again to develop into a self-supporting and prosperous state, free to play a role in the world that is worthy of her great heritage.

Such common ties and interest cannot but create among us an atmosphere and change of thought. In such an atmosphere, I feel free to speak about interesting facts frankly and informally.

It has been almost 3,000 years since there began to glow in Greece the sparks of a new culture, based on Democracy, tolerance, and respect for the dignity and rights of men. These sparks gradually developed into a flame of such brightness that it penetrated all the recesses of the then-known world. During the vicissitudes of the intervening centuries, light emanated from Greece.

Nevertheless, it has never been completely smothered. Since the Greek liberation about a century and a quarter ago, it has been gaining in brightness. Even during the centuries when Greece was deprived of her political independence, the Greek people, by their stubborn adherence to the principles of Democracy and by their sustained struggle for freedom, continued to set an inspiring example for liberty-loving people everywhere. It would be a tragedy if in our generation that this flame, which has survived through the millennia, should be finally extinguished.

JOHN'S STORY

Editor's Note: John C. Papademetriou started writing his life story while stationed as an Army Medical Combat Technician (M.C.T) in Korea. He died at the front lines on May 12, 1951, before he completed his project. After John's death, his Army friend, George C. MacNee, saved John's story by writing it out by hand. He also wrote a moving tribute to John. MacNee's handwritten version is transcribed here.

MOLINE'S MOUNTAIN "DOCTOR"

George C. MacNee

John C. Papademetriou, now with the Second Division Medics in Korea, is no doctor. He is no physician, but it is said here that no medical practitioner was ever held in higher esteem for the ability with which he serves his patients.

The Moline, Illinois M.C.T.'s duty is to render medical assistance to our men at the front lines, but he also derives considerable satisfaction by treating the P.O.W.s and the sick and wounded civilians on his own.

M.C.T. John C. Papademetriou joined the division last February and was attached to the medical company of the Ninth Regiment. He was assigned the duty of treating and caring for the G.I.s, P.O.W.s, as well as the long-suffering civilians throughout the mountains and villages of Korea.

The G.I. "doctor" best enjoys his work with the men at the front lines. In turn, they have grown to love him.

He is called in on a new case every day: to treat a fever that almost all Koreans have; to bandage the wound of one of our heroic men in the front lines; to administer penicillin for a sore throat; or to set a broken leg.

Ironically enough, the American soldier with the long Greek name only became interested in the medics when he joined the armed forces, and the only medical knowledge he had was that knowledge that he received in the Army. "Doc the Greek" had his medical training at the Medical Field Service School, Fort Sam Houston, San Antonio, Texas.

He must have studied hard to know all that Dr. Kozier said he knew at the collecting station.

We all know "Doc the Greek" as a great medical helper, and the first friend of all who know him.

PREFACE

This is a real story. I wrote it in the front lines of Korea. After the battles were over and I had any spare time, I spent every minute writing this story.

This is a story written with fear, waiting for death minute by minute. But I made it so far and I hope that the war shall be over soon so that I may complete the second edition of my adventures in the front lines of Korea.

John C. Papademetriou
Medical Combat Technician
R.A. 17282405

MY STORY

On February 28, 1951, I joined the Second Division in Korea.

Now, I am in the combat zone. I have to think back to my training and try to remember all that I had learned. There is no time for training now. This is the real thing.

I am attached to Company B of the Ninth Infantry Regiment as a medical combat technician. I must be prepared to take care of any kind of accident, the wounded, the sick, and those killed in action.

When I was attached to the medical company of the Ninth Regiment, my company commander asked me what I would like to do best: to stay at the collecting station as an assistant in surgery or to take a place at the front with the medical combat technicians. I could hardly answer that because I wanted to serve in both places. As I could only do one job, I asked him to let me think it over overnight.

The next morning, he asked me again. He said, "Well, Pfc. Papademetriou, did you make up your mind yet?"

After thinking a while, I answered, "Yes, sir. I want to serve with the medical combat team."

The captain was taken by surprise, and he didn't know what to say. Finally, he said, "But John, it's better for you here. You are safer, there is more food, and it's warm and everything. This is more like home."

I said, "I'm sorry, sir. My duty is where they need me, not where it is better for me. Only women like to stay where it is warm. I am a man of Greek peasant stock, toughened by the cold and hunger during the Second World War in Greece."

The captain then turned his face the other way. He said, "Yeah. I guess you're all right," and walked into his tent.

The next morning, the captain called me to his office. I went near the door and asked, "May I come in please, sir."

The captain answered, "Yes, John. Come right in, and sit down." There was a little chair, the kind that is used in the combat zones.

I said, "I understand that you wanted to see me. Is that right, Sir?"

"Yes, I do," he said. "The reason I ask you to stay here is because you have a good score on your record. Over the past four days that you have been here, you have tried to do the best you can with the knowledge you have as a medic. There are many here who really know how to do it, and have much more medical training, but they don't do it unless I tell them to do it."

"Well, sir," I said, "that is up to the individual. We take orders from the doctor because we are not doctors."

"Yes, but those little things that you do don't need orders from the doctors. You had that all in medical training," he replied.

Then, I didn't know what to say.

He looked at me but I couldn't look at him. I knew he wanted me to stay there, but he didn't say anything. He wanted me to say it.

"If there is an order to stay here, sir, I will follow it, but if it is up to me, I would rather like to go there, because they need me, sir," I told him.

"I guess I can't make you stay here, but I want to wish you good luck." He gave me his hand to shake. "Be careful now," he said as we stood up from the little table.

As I was leaving, I answered, "I'll do my best."

After a while, we had chow. A little later, we had a formation. The 1st sergeant, a tall, dark master sergeant who was about 32 years old, called my name and told me that I was going to the First Battalion Aid Station.

After the formation, the 1st sergeant introduced me to Master Sgt. Frank, who was in charge of the medics of the First Battalion Aid Station. Sgt. Frank was a short, fat man with big glasses. He was waiting for me with a litter jeep. Sgt. Frank then told me to take my full field pack, my cargo pack, and my duffel bag, and put them in the jeep. After we got in the jeep, we drove up to the aid station.

While we were in the jeep, we started a conversation. I asked him where he was from. He said, "I am from San Antonio, Texas. Where are you from?"

"I'm from Moline, Illinois," I said, "but I had my medical training at Fort Sam Houston, Texas."

"Well," he said, "that's something. How is my old city? Did you like San Antonio? How long were you stationed there? My wife lives there, and I lived there all my life. What is your name again?"

"My name is Papademetriou," I said.

"What? Say that again," he said.

"My name is hard to remember, so just call me John," I said.

"Tell me, John, what nationality are you?" he asked.

"I'm a Greek," I replied.

"No wonder why I can't pronounce your name," Sgt. Frank told me. "Tell me about yourself, John. Do you live in the States, or did you come straight from Greece?"

I replied, "I came from Greece about three years ago."

"Well, tell me, how did you happen to come to America, and join the Army? Tell the story, John," he said.

Then, I started to tell him the story. All the while we were on the jeep, and he listened very closely.

"It's a long story, and I'm only going to tell you the highlights because it would take months to tell it all," I said.

"Yes, go on," Sgt. Frank replied.

"I was born in a little village of Greece, called Petralona. There are only about 200 homes. It is a very small community, but very good, clean, and ornamented with the most beautiful things that nature has placed on earth.

"My father, who is now a priest of St. George Greek Orthodox Church in Moline, Illinois, was a schoolteacher and priest of the community Nostino, Karpenisi. He used to visit us every weekend. There was my mother, Ourania, my oldest brother, Spiro, my sister, Olga, and my younger brothers, George, Evangelos, and Alkiviades. We stayed with my grandfather, George D. Papademetriou, in Petralona. Spiro, Olga, and I went to school there.

"Later, we moved to a town called Hohlia, where we stayed until before we came to the United States."

"Yes, but for what reason did you come to the United States? Sgt. Frank asked.

"Wait a minute. I'm getting to that," I said.

"My father was a priest and teacher, as I told you before. The Greek communities in America were short of priests, so the Greek Orthodox Archdiocese of America requested from the Archdiocese in Athens to send missionaries to America. The Archbishop of Athens asked for volunteers. Many volunteered, and my father was one of them.

"This was before the War, and my father came to America alone. Then, the War broke out, and we didn't know whether my father was alive or dead.

"After the War, my father wrote to us that he had become an American citizen, and that he was going to bring us over. That was in 1946. My father wrote to us to go and stay in Athens until the necessary papers were completed to bring us to America.

"We stayed in Athens six months. One day in January 1947 (I don't remember the exact date), we took some of our belongings and called a taxi to take us to Piraeus, the port of Athens. There were about a thousand people there to say good-bye to their relatives and friends who were leaving for America. Many of my buddies from Athens came to say good-bye.

"We got on board ship, the Saturnia, and we arrived in America on February 5, 1947. We debarked at New York City, where we were surprised at all the tall buildings. We admired them very much. We also have many beautiful buildings in Greece, made of marble, but nothing that tall."

"Yes, we have the best," Sgt. Frank said.

But I said, "No, you have the most, but not the best."

Then, we started to argue, but I cut him off by saying, "O.K, quit arguing if you want to hear the rest of my story."

He said, "All right, you win."

"My father, who waited to receive us, took us to a hotel, and we stayed overnight. In the morning, he took us to Grand Central Terminal, and we got on the train for Moline, Illinois. We arrived in Moline in the middle of the night on February 7, 1947.

"We stayed at the LeClair Hotel for a week until we rented a house near the church where my father serves."

"Well, we're here at the Aid Station," Sgt. Frank said.

We got out of the jeep, and we went across a stream where the doctor and the other medics were. Sgt. Frank introduced me to all of them, but I can hardly remember their names now.

I was supposed to go up in the line the same day, but Sgt. Frank was interested in my story, and he asked the doctor if I could stay at the Aid Station overnight. The doctor said it was all right, so Sgt. Frank asked me to stay overnight.

Of course, I had to accept because it was almost chow time. Soon, it would be dark, and I probably couldn't see my fingers in front of my face that night. It was cloudy, and there was about two feet of snow on the ground. I told Sgt. Frank that I would stay there that night.

After we had supper, Sgt. Frank said, "Let's go to my tent. You're probably tired."

"I'm not as tired as you think," I answered. But we went to his tent anyway.

He had a private tent, but we could both sleep in it. He also had a little stove, but it was not burning.

Sgt. Frank excused himself to get some gas for the stove. "It's too cold here in Korea," he said.

"Yes, go ahead," I said.

After Sgt. Frank made the fire, we made our bunks to sleep. After we got in our sleeping bags, Sgt. Frank asked me to continue my story while he lit a white candle.

"Well, what happened after you got to your new house?" Sgt. Frank asked.

"I spent almost three years in Moline with my parents, until I came into the Army."

Sgt. Frank asked, "How did you come into the Army? Did you enlist, or were you drafted?"

"I enlisted," I said.

"Tell me all about it. How did it happen? I like to listen to you. I'm very interested in your story. Tell me about your job in Moline. Did you like it? And, did you have many friends?"

"Oh, yes. Of course, I have many friends," I said.

"Well, tell me about it," Sgt. Frank said.

"When I came to Moline, I couldn't speak English at all. I didn't even know the alphabet."

"How do you speak such good English now?" Sgt. Frank asked.

"I went to school," I answered. "Three months after we arrived in Moline, my father asked us if we wanted to go to school. At the same time, he had already made an appointment on the telephone with the Superintendent of Schools for the next day.

"The next day, we went up a hill to the Superintendent's office. The Superintendent was a Mr. Jardine. (I met him again before I came overseas.) When we entered the door of the building to Mr. Jardine's office, a young lady asked, 'Could I help you?' My father said, 'Yes, we would like to see Mr. Jardine.'

"In a few minutes, Mr. Jardine and his secretary appeared, and he took us to his office.

"I can remember exactly how we were sitting, too. First, there was Mr. Jardine, then my father, Rev. Constantine Papademetriou, then my sister, Olga, my brothers, George, Evangelos, and the youngest, Alkiviades."

"Gosh, how many brothers do you have?" Sgt. Frank asked.

"We are five brothers, and one sister," I said.

"But you mentioned only four."

"Yes, because my oldest brother, Spiro, was going to Theological Seminary near Boston, Mass.

"It was very funny how Mr. Jardine and my father were talking, and we couldn't understand a thing.

"Finally, the conversation was over. They had decided what classes we were to attend. My sister and I had to start at the seventh grade, and my younger brothers were sent to grammar school.

"All the students at school were very interested in us. They wished to help us, and they did, too.

"After three weeks at Calvin Coolidge Junior High School, I was transferred to the eighth grade, but my sister stopped going. By June, I had learned enough English to work on my school problems.

"Then, Mr. Condon, the school principal, gave me a test, and I passed. So, I graduated to tenth grade at the end of June 1947.

"That summer, I started working for the Tri-City Packing Co. in Silvis, Illinois.

"In the morning from 8 to 10, I attended Senior High School classes in summer school, and from 12 to 9, I worked in the grocery store. I graduated from Moline Senior High School in June 1950.

"On July 23 of that year, I went to Davenport, Iowa. I took a test for the Army. The Section Recruiting Commander Lt. Harvey Cox helped me on it.

"When I returned home, I told my mother, but she didn't like it. When I asked my father about it, he said, 'If that's what you want, go ahead.'

"The next day, I said good-bye to my father and brothers, and kissed my mother. Then, I got on the bus, and went back to the recruiting station. Lt. Cox was waiting for me. He called all the Quad City newspapers. They came and took our pictures, and wrote a story about me.

"The same day, I got on the train, and left Davenport for Des Moines, Iowa. I arrived there at five o'clock in the evening at the recruiting station. I was given meal tickets, and a ticket for one night at a hotel.

"In the morning of July 25, I went to the recruiting station where I took my final physical. The Commander of the Des Moines Recruiting Station swore us in. There were about 35 of us there, and he told us that we were in the Army, and that we were no longer civilians.

"After the speech, we went into the next room, where a sergeant gave us tickets to go to a movie. Later, we went back to the hotel to sleep because the next day we had to travel.

"The next morning, we went back to the recruiting station, and again received meal tickets, but this time with our train tickets and our records. I was put in charge of the 35 men, so I had to carry all the tickets and the records.

"We traveled all night. The next day, we arrived in Los Angeles, California. There, we changed and took a train for Fort Ord.

"We had a three hour wait between trains, so I asked the boys to stick together. They all agreed, and we saw some nice places in Los Angeles.

"We arrived at Fort Ord early in the morning. An Army bus took us to an area where we were processed. After processing, we had chow, and then we were attached to L Company, 12 Regiment of the 4th Division.

"The first week, I didn't like it at all because they worked us so hard that I hated them."

Sgt. Frank then asked what kind of work they had me do.

"Well, they didn't give it only to me, but to all the others, too. We didn't have any military training at all the first week, only K.P., clean the streets, police the areas, and G.I. the floors. There wasn't a moment when they didn't have us doing something.

"Anyway, after six weeks of basic, and six weeks of Infantry training, I received my orders to report to the M.R.T.C. Branch of the Medical Field Service School, at Fort Sam Houston, San Antonio, Texas, for my medical training.

"I had a good time at Fort Sam Houston. There was a Greek Orthodox Church nearby, and I went every Sunday. The Rev. John Tographas asked me to be his helper, and I was extremely happy to assist the Rev. He asked me to make a speech. The title of it was "We are Creators." I attended meetings every Sunday night in the church dining hall. The purpose of the meetings was to teach the true gospel.

"I will never forget New Year's Eve, when there was a dance, where many Greek boys and girls had gathered. We danced both Greek and American, and had a wonderful time all night. It was there that I met a very beautiful girl. Her name was Ernino. She writes to me very often too.

"The next day, Master Sgt. Moffet called our names, and gave us the Order Sheet (that was on January 1) to report to Camp Stoneman, California on January 19. So, I went home for ten days. When I arrived there, I surprised my mother who leaped upon me, and kissed me at the same time. I hadn't let them know that I was coming. I had a wonderful time for the ten days I was there.

"On January 19, I arrived at Camp Stoneman, and was stationed there for 13 days. There, I was issued all new clothes, shoes, and equipment.

"While there, I visited the Greek communities in San Francisco, and Oakland.

"On February 2nd, we boarded the troop ship General Howze. For five days, most of us were seasick.

"I met some buddies on the ship, some who were from Ft. Ord, and some from Ft. Sam Houston. One was Pvt. Robert Nicholson, and the other was Vasily Matchakevich, who was from Russia. He came to the U.S. a year and a half ago. He was working with a Soviet mission when he crossed into the American zone, and went to work for the U.S. troops in Germany. Later, he came to the U.S. and settled in Los Angeles. He was here 8 months when he joined the Army.

"There were also many others: John Nibles, Adonio, Moloy, Plamanchare, and more I can't remember.

"Even though we were seasick, we still had to work, K.P., sanitation, P.X., and so forth. I was put to work in the dispensary, giving all kinds of shots.

"We arrived in the beautiful port of Yokohama, Japan, where top Army leaders and music welcomed us. We debarked and boarded trains where we were hardly seated when the mail was passed to us. It was waiting for us before we got there.

"About fifteen of us were sent to Tokyo General Hospital. I was glad to go there, but I was transferred again because so many Korean veterans were coming there, so I was sent to Korea.

"The next morning, a short blond captain told us we were going to Camp Drake. Now let me tell you about Camp Drake. It's a very nice place, Frank."

"Yes, I know," Sgt. Frank answered. "I was there too before I came to Korea."

"Let me tell you about my activities there."

"Yes, go on," he said.

"We came to what they call Provision Company. They have big barracks, each of which holds 300 men. They are clean and nice, and they have Japanese employees, who keep them clean."

"I wouldn't mind staying in Japan," Sgt. Frank said.

"Yes, I wouldn't either," I replied.

"Then what happened?" Sgt. Frank asked.

"The first day, we turned in all of our equipment and drew new ones. All kinds of winter clothing that we would need in Korea. The next day, the Sgt. told us that we could go anywhere we wanted. I decided to go to Tokyo to see some friends before I left for Korea. They were Greek casualties from Korea.

"I spent about 8 hours with those Greek wounded. There were about 15 of them and they all told me to be careful because it was very bad there.

"I thanked them and told them, 'I will.'

"I returned to Camp Drake at 5 o'clock and had chow. Later that night, I went to the service club to a dance. I didn't know anyone, and was not enjoying myself. As I got up to leave, a Japanese girl came over and spoke to me.

" 'Hello,' she said, with a smile on her lips. She was the prettiest Japanese girl I had seen in Japan.

" 'Hello,' I answered.

" 'Why do you want to leave us? Don't you like us? Don't you like our music, or our company? Sit down. I'd like to talk to you, so maybe then you'll like us.'

"She spoke very good English, and I could understand her.

" 'Well,' I said, 'it's not that I don't like you, or your very nice music, and all the good things that you do for us, but something else bothers me.'

" 'If you don't mind, may I ask what it is?' she asked. 'Is it that you are far from home, or your girl? You don't have to worry about that, because you will find a good home and a girl here in Japan.'

" 'No, it isn't that,' I said.

" 'Then, what is it?' she asked.

" 'Well, when you go to an affair by yourself, and don't know anyone, you don't feel very happy.'

" 'Maybe so, but the Japanese are very happy to meet the G.I.'s,' she said.

"After we had a drink, I asked her for a dance, and we danced until the dance was over. Then, I went to the barracks to sleep.

"The next three days, I only went to the movies, went to the P.X., or slept. I didn't feel like doing anything. I would rather sleep than run around.

"On the fifth day, I got on the train, and went 40 miles south of Camp Drake to a camp, and stayed one day. There, we boarded a Japanese boat, and came to Korea. We debarked in Pusan. We got on a train, and arrived at the 2nd Division Headquarters. From there, they sent us to the 9th Infantry Regimental Headquarters, and then to the medical company. Now, I'm on my way to the Medical Combat team."

"Well, that was very interesting, but now let's get some sleep, because we get up early tomorrow."

"Yes, Sgt, good night," I said.

"Good night," he replied.

This is the end of the first of a series. Another installment (a better one, I hope) will follow in the near future. The subject will be my experience in a combat zone.

****

George C. MacNee comments: John never completed what he set out to do. His duties never gave him any spare time. He fell on May 12, 1951, during the big communist push. Another cross bearing "Died in Action." In the course of human endeavor, many fall by the wayside.

LETTERS

Fort Ord, Monterey, California
July 29, 1950

Dear George [one of John's brothers],
Really, I had a very good time on my trip through to the camp. George, write to me some time whenever you have time. Be attentive to our parents because later you will change your mind. I will not [be able to] write a letter to you as [much] as I write to all of you now. Try to do your best with school next year, and write to me all the news from Moline.
With a brother's lov[ing] kiss, John P.

[Translated from the Greek]
Fort Ord, Monterey, California
September 11, 1950

Dear Alki [one of John's brothers],
Since I left, I did not write to you because I have a lot of work to do in the Army. In any event, you should listen to your parents, and go regularly to school now that it is starting. Don't forget to write to me some time. The photograph [on the postcard] shows the barracks in which we live.
With love, John

[Translated from the Greek]
Fort Sam Houston, San Antonio, Texas
October 30, 1950

Dear Mother,
Greetings. I'm fine. I hope the same for all of you. They stationed me again to the same address [San Antonio, Texas]. Please write to me frequently. Tomorrow, I am going to go to church with some other Greek guys.

I'll write the details to you tomorrow.

The photograph on this postcard is of the hospital where I take classes [Brooke Hospital Center Headquarters, Fort Sam Houston]. It's in the center of town.

With love, John

[Translated from the Greek]
Camp Stoneman, Pittsburg, California
January 25, 1951

Dear brothers George, Vageli, and Alki:
I'm fine and hope the same for you. A couple of days ago on Sunday, I went to San Francisco to church. I had a nice time.

Write to me frequently. When I leave from here, I don't know where we will go. But write to me and I will receive your letters.

I think that all of us medics will leave from here, I believe by air. [They went by ship. See letter dated February 18, 1951.] I will write to you when I find a chance. Give my regards to everyone.

John Papademetriou

[Translated from the Greek]
San Antonio, Texas
January 31, 1951

Dear George,

Greetings. I received your letter and was glad about your good health. I am also fine, thank God. George, I am leaving tomorrow from here, for where I don't know.

My address will be as follows: [Army Post Office in San Francisco]. Don't expect to receive a letter from me if you don't first reply immediately. I also wrote to the others in New York, but did not receive a response.

George, please write to me frequently. Wherever I am stationed, I will write to you immediately. I sent a large photo previously. Please frame it. The other photo I sent you last summer, please send it to Greece.

To finish, please give my regards to Father, Vageli [one of John's brothers], and Alki.

With brotherly love, John

P.S. If you find a letter, put it in a suitcase and don't lose it.

Sea of Japan
February 14, 1951

Dear Spiro and Metaxia [John's oldest brother and his wife]:

We just have crossed the Sea of Japan, and you know there is a one day difference between here and the States. Today, February 12, became the 14th. Now coming this way we win one day, but on our returning to the States we shall lose one.

Write to me all the story of how Mother came and left again. I hope she came in good condition.

Love, John (Brother)

[Translated from the Greek]
Yokohoma, Japan
February 18, 1951

Respected parents and beloved siblings,
With God's help, we arrived safely. We had a good trip. I didn't throw up at all, as my work did not let the ocean upset me, or just a little bit.

I will try to write you tomorrow, but don't forget to write to me. I send my love.

John Papademetriou

P.S. The picture [on the postcard showing the U.S.N.S. General R.L. Howze] is of the ship on which we traveled.

Korea
February 30, 1951

Dear Spiro and Metaxia:
Today I came to Korea where, from a far distance, I hear the fire of our delight.

I had a very nice time in Japan. It's very poor, people live very dirty, but they are very nice people. I was in Tokyo, Nagasaki, Yokohama, and various other places of which I can't think their names.

Well, I guess I can't think of anything else to write, so I might as well sign off. Please give my regards to all relatives and friends that may concern you.

Love,
John C. Papademetriou

[Translated from the Greek]
Korea
March 2, 1951

Dear George,

Greetings. I am now near the front lines, 10 miles south. I will probably remain here because as things go on they need a Greek interpreter. They told me that it is likely for me to remain here, but I'm not sure. It is not likely that I will go to the front line. Up to now, I have not met any Greeks. They are about 4 miles in front of here, but from time to time, Greek officers pass by and they don't have an interpreter.

George, please write to me frequently so I can learn what is happening to you. How is Mother? Did she return from New York? How is Nikki [the baby daughter of John's sister Olga]?

I have not written to anyone in Greece yet. I'll write as soon as I am free. George, please don't believe what they are saying about things here. Things are not like they are saying. We are fine, except that it is a little cold.

Give my regards to Father and Mother, Vageli and Alki. Alki should listen to Mother and not make her worry.

I'm waiting for your letter.

With brotherly love, John

Korea
March 4, 1951

Dear Steve [the husband of John's sister Olga],

Now I'm about 300 yds south of the first line. I'm at the clearing station. I wish to go up there and see the fight, but I can't do it.

It does not sound as bad as they express it in the States. We are doing wonderful right now. Our air force all day throws candy at the enemy. At night, we have the tanks.

Well, Steve, I guess I don't have much to tell except that I am well and safe. Give my regards to Olga and kisses to Nikki.

Love,
Your brother-in-law
John Papademetriou

Korea
March 6, 1951
Dear George,

How do you do, George? How are things in Moline? Did the newspaper announce that I am serving in Korea? If so, send me a clipping.

Well George, I'm not in the front lines and I never will be, but I would like to get up there some time just to see.

We have cold weather. At night, it snows and during the day it freezes. Soon that terrible cold will be over, so don't worry about it.

How about you, George? Have you been drafted? Write to me about it, and please don't make Mother worry.

Love, John

Korea
March 6, 1951
Dear Metaxia,

How you doing, Sister? How is my old beloved Brother? Is he working? What are you doing? Is Mother still at New York? Write to me big, nice letters like you used to. Why don't you do it no more, Sister? I know that you are busy, but write sometime.

O, I have good times here at the collecting station, don't worry about me. Just look and find a nice bride. When I come back to the States, I'm going to get married. That's the good life to think of. I just trust you, you find the bride, and I'll do the job. I want [her] to be from New York, a Yankee.

Well, Metaxia, here we have snow and cold, but it will be over soon. The Koreans fear the GI's as the Italians used to [fear the Greeks in] Albania. They run away when they hear GI. The Chinese have disappeared from the front lines.

Please, when you write to me, write to me air mail because by ship I don't get it for 3 months.

You know, right now it's time to eat, so I must sign off. Please give my hearty regards to Spiro and all those friends who may concern you.

With brotherly love,
John C. Papademetriou

Korea
March 13, 1951
Dear Spiro:

Spiro, how do you do, boy? How is my lovely sister Metaxia? Is she now working? Well today is a sunny, beautiful day. There's snow on the ground, but anyway today it's warmer than the other days.

I have a very good job, Spiro. I know now you worry because I am in Korea. Well, it's nothing to worry about. I'm a field medical technician, and I always go behind our glorious troops.

They call me Doc and they respect me much more than they did in the hospital. It's why I do like it here better. I do much walking, but so what. That's nothing. I want you to write to Mother regularly and tell her that I'm well settled. I may not have much time to write as often as I want, but you do. So please, write to Mother.

Mail I don't get. What's going on, I don't know. As they tell me, the post office in Korea is slow, so I don't worry too much.

Please give my regards to Metaxia and all those who ask for me.
Love, Brother
John C. Papademetriou

Korea
March 21, 1951

Dear Brother & Sister [Spiro and Metaxia]:
Today is a sunny day. I am in a Korean village where the sun warms me up. We just have come back about 15 miles from the line. Here it's very good, but [it's] not stateside.

I have a long time to hear from all of you. Sometimes, I worry, but again I know I have to wait for some time. Here in Korea, I know people with whom we came together and they already got their mail.

Now Easter comes near, and I just happen to think again of ...[rest of letter is missing].

Korea
March 24, 1951
Dear Steve,
I am greatly well. I wish the same for you.

Today we went far up, as far as the 38th parallel, and returned 10 miles back now. We had fun while we had the infantry beside us.

Well Steve, I ask you to do me a favor, which is very simple. I have a buddy here in Korea who has a 35 mm camera, and I want you to send me two rolls of 35 mm Kodachrome daylight type 20 exposure. Please do not be careless. Mail them as soon as you get my letter. I'm sure the drug store in New York is open day and night, so please send them to me airmail and insured. I thank you very much, and appreciate the work you have done for me. Also, write to me how much it will cost so I can send you the money. My hearty regards to Olga.

Love, John

Korea
March 29, 1951
Dear Brother George,

How is everything back home? Well today, I got your letter, and I was joyful to hear about your good health. That was the first letter I got since I came to Korea, it's why I do want you to write to me by airmail.

Well George, we now are far away back from the lines, and we shall go farther back for three weeks. I notice in your letter that you are going to be drafted. If you ask my advice, I would tell you to try to enlist in the Navy Reserves. If you do not make it, then try the Army Enlisted Reserves. Do not feel bad because it is not as bad as you think. If you come in [the Service], you will find that out, so please do not worry about it. May God look down upon us and protect us.

Ending my letter, I wish you the best, and give my regards to Dad and Mom, and Vageli and Alki. Write to me soon with news from Moline.

Love, John

Korea
April 4, 1951
Dear Brother and Sister:

I received your card for my birthday, and I thank you very much. Spiro has always been very kind to me, and Metaxia too, too much. But Metaxia has not been writing to me lately. You know, I love you both so much. I would like to be near you, but my job is here, my duty. So I pray to God for peace, and after 6-8 months, I'll be back.

Last March 25, I went to the Greek Church about 40 miles away from here. There was a bishop, and I talked with him. But I didn't stay.

Well, I have to go now. So I better sign off. If Mother is with you, tell her not to worry. I want her not to worry because I want to see her again when I come back, and if [illegible] I won't.

Give my regards to all in N.Y.

Love,
John Papademetriou

[Translated from the Greek]
Korea
April 4, 1951
Dear Olga, Greetings:

I received your letters, and I thank you very much for your good wishes and I send you all my thanks and all the most beautiful love to be with you.

I imagine Nikki's tears, as you write me. Tell her I will return in 6-8 months. I wrote you a few days ago to send me 2 rolls of 35 mm film. I want to take some photographs now that a friend of mine is here who has a camera. I ask you if you can send it as soon as you can because I don't know how long he will be here. Send it to me and write to me how much it costs. I will send you whatever it costs by money order.

Don't worry for me. I'm fine. Give kisses to Nikki and regards to beloved Steve.

With brotherly love,
John

Korea
April 18, 1951

Dear Miss Hendee [Marjory Hendee, John's teacher at Moline High School],
Received your letter and the newspaper clipping, and enjoyed it very much. Jackie is very cute (as you say in the newspaper clipping!). Tell her Hello if you see her around.
Well Miss Hendee, there I am again writing poetry. I finished my eighth one just now. I'm sending them home, because when or if I'll come back I shall use them.
I have been a medical combat technician near almost 150 yards behind the lines, and now while my unit is resting somewhere behind the 38th parallel, I came to the C.Y. Dental Clinic for a little more practice. I have one and a half more weeks to go here, and then I shall return back to my unit. I'm just thinking back to when I was at Moline High, and I do wish to be there again, even though I have been home sick.
About that Moline you have written about, I have been looking for a Moliner for a long time, but as yet I have only met a buddy I knew who worked at the factory of John Deere and Co. in Moline. He is from St. Louis. I only saw him as I was passing by on the jeep. He was looking at me, and I was looking at him until we finally found ourselves knowing each other. He just came over. I felt sorry because I did not have a long time to talk with him, only a few minutes.
Ending my letter, I again express my regards to the teachers I had classes with (that you know) and all my friends in your classes. Especially, I do wish you a very good summer vacation of the year 1951.
Sincerely,
John C. Papademetriou
M.C.T. Med. Department
Army of the U.S.

Korea
April 24, 1951

Dear Spiro:

Today, I sent you some poems I have written here in Korea. I want you to call up the *Atlantis* [Greek-American newspaper] and work with them. I'm sure they will accept it. It won't be bad to try it anyway. It can be a pamphlet and a good one, too.

If there are any contracts that must be signed by me only, please send me their address. I'll write to them too. But be sure that you also will call them up and tell them to send a reporter or a publisher to talk with you. You know about that better than me. Also, you may put on the cover the picture I sent you from Camp Stoneman. You may use any of my pictures you have, but not of anyone else.

Please call them soon and write to me with whom you are going to work, send me his name and address. I also sent you an article written by Captain McNee. That must be in it too.

Write me soon.

Love,

John

Korea
May 10, 1951 (postmarked May 13, 1951)

Dear George,

I hope this letter will find you well. I am well for the moment.

It is now getting a little worse than it was, but it will soon be settled. Right now, I'm up in the front line. Tomorrow, I return back. Please don't tell Mama that I am in the front line.

Please write to me about everything there. If you saw pictures in the newspaper, send them to me. I would like to see them

Write to me about how you are getting along in school, and all about your behavior.

Love, your brother, John

Editor's Note: John was killed in action on May 12, 1951.

Secretary of the Army
Washington, D.C.
11 June 1951

My dear Mr. [Rev. Constantine] Papademetriou [John's father]:

At the request of the President, I write to inform you that the Purple Heart has been awarded posthumously to your son, Private First Class John C. Papademetriou, Army Medical Service, who sacrificed his life in Korea.

Little that we can do or say will console you for the death of your loved one. We profoundly appreciate the greatness of your loss, for in a very real sense the loss suffered by any of us is a loss shared by all of us. When the medal, which you will soon receive, reaches you, I want you to know that with it goes my sincerest sympathy and the hope that time and victory of our cause will finally lighten the burden of your grief.

Sincerely yours,
Frank Pace, Jr.
Secretary of the Army

ESSAYS

LIFE IN GREECE

THE SENSES:
SIGHT, SOUND, FEEL, SMELL, AND TASTE

Sight: My Grade School in Greece

Our school was small but beautiful. It was made of snow-white marble stone in 1902. Outside, there was a big yard that was used only by students for gymnasium and playing. During the summer, everyone used the yard for recreation and dances.

Inside, the school had only five rooms. The first and second rooms were used as regular classrooms. The third room was used as a cafeteria. The school also had rest rooms, and a study hall or library. The student desks were bigger and wider than the desks here. Under the desks were lockers used only for school supplies. For other things like coats or overshoes, we had a special room. Student dramatic players used the big auditorium.

Sound: The Forest

During summer vacation, when I completed my work every afternoon at five o'clock, I went to a place that is about three or four blocks from the high school. There, I lay down, and sometimes I read some books and studied.

Usually, there were not many people around during that time, and it had a natural feeling. The trees rustled their leaves. Quite a few birds sang. Many times when I went to the forest during the summer, I felt happier than I felt most of the time in the city. The country out there had a clean nature, which gave me more life.

Feeling: Health

When my family and I came from Greece, we were not very healthy because of the War's suffering. We looked thin and yellow, especially I, who went through so much suffering in the War, and my mother, whose heart was often troubled. Now we are better. Why? Because we have food, a warm house, and other things that we need.

A week ago, my brother, George, went to the hospital for his appendix. He told me he didn't understand at all what was happening. He still had a good time with the nurses in there. He thinks it is easier in America to have operations, and to find doctors. We feel better now than before.

Smell and Taste: My Mother's Food

A few days ago, my mother cooked nice food. She took eggs, added some Greek cheese, and fried them. I was coming home from school. When I came to the front door, the delicious smell of the eggs came to my nose. My mother told me to sit down. As I sat down, my mother brought me that naturally good food. I ate it with much pleasure. After I finished, I asked my mother if I there could be anybody who would not be interested in such food. She answered, "Nobody. Yes, nobody, because it was made with my hands." I said, "Truly, Mother, you are good and sweet. Everything you make is as good as you." And she smiled.

MY GRANDFATHER

My grandfather is now 87 years old. He is still alive in Greece, and is very active. [Editor's Note: John's grandfather died in 1959.] His great reputation is well known in his territory in Greece.

How he looked in his youth, I don't know exactly. As my parents describe him, I think I can picture him. When he was young, before his marriage, he was beautiful. His hair was curly, his body was straight, and his eyes were smart. He was a fatherless orphan since he was twelve years old.

At the age of 23, he married Miss Paraskevi Tsirigas from the town of Vracha. After his marriage, he was respected in his town of Petralona. He was elected mayor. He was also president of the St. Nicholas Church.

My grandfather came to the United States early in his life, but he did not stay. He was in the United States only five years. As he told me, he worked hard to make some money, but he also had a good time.

When my grandfather returned to Greece from America, he opened his own business, with the money he made in America. He opened a very good general store, the only one in the town. He also bought many acres of farmland, and many animals.

Now, my grandfather does not look very good. He looks old, but not as old as his age. His formerly handsome and straight body has bent over. His formerly curly hair has fallen out. His formerly white, clean face is wrinkled.

My grandfather likes to play the clarinet, and the violin. When he sings, his voice can no longer follow the note keys of the western music because he is weak. As he told me, when he was young, he was a very good singer. I wish to express my appreciation for the opportunity to sing with him while he is still alive.

WHAT HAPPENED TO ME ON JULY 15, 1938

The summer of 1938 was very warm in our region. One day, I remember it was July 15, stuck out because it was hotter than the other days of that summer.

At about six o'clock, I left the town, and went by myself to the hill which is only a few feet outside of our town. I lay under a green tree for a while. The fresh air struck me and made me feel good.

Later, it became dark, but what was there for me to fear? Not a thing. But there I was, afraid. The dark night brought ideas to my mind. The trees moved their branches and their leaves made a little noise. I thought I was lost, lost forever. I started to walk. Where was I going? I didn't know. After a while, I stopped walking and started to cry, but nobody heard me. I called, "Mama, mama," but my mother could not hear me because she was too far away. I started to wonder why I hadn't asked my mother to come.

Then, I started to run, run, and run some more. As I ran, I came to a goat keeper's barn. I called, "Eh! Is anybody here?" Nobody answered. I called again and again. After some time, I saw a young man who was about 21 years old.

He asked me, "What do you want?"

I answered, "Please, can you help me?"

He asked, "What happened?"

"I lost my way, and I am afraid of staying out here. Please take me back to my mother."

"Well," he said, "come in to have a little rest first, and then you can go."

"Yes, I would be glad," I answered. I went in and we stayed there for about two hours. Then, he held a flashlight and took me home. I was very happy because I returned home after I thought that I was lost.

The young man left, and I was now among my mother and brothers. My mother asked me where I went that evening. What could I tell her? I was frightened that she would ask me why I went out without asking. Yet, I thought that I should tell her, so I did. As I sat down, I explained the whole story to my family.

My mother laughed and told me, "I'm telling you once and for all. If you want to look out for your own good, and not get lost again, you have to ask me first before you go anywhere."

I only answered "yes." That was a good lesson for me at the young age of nine years old.

LIFE IN THE CONCENTRATION CAMP

My life has been in many storms since I was born. The most terrible story begins in 1940, when I was a student in a little school outside of my town. That year, the great tragedy for all of us in the town was when we heard that the Italians had started the war against Greece. Soon afterwards, airplanes covered our town with bombs.

But I wish to come to the most emotional part of my story. It makes me cry sometimes when I remember it.

This emotion is brought on by memories of the six months of my very young life spent in the concentration camp in 1941. That experience brought me to a point of Life or Death. I suffered, but I was not the only one who suffered. Many of my fellow countrymen also did. God, who always helps young people with their needs, also helped me through that great sacrifice.

Here is a description of what happened when I was in the camp. Everyday, we would get up at eight o'clock. The Italians would put us in lines. Later, we would get our lunch. You could not feed a chicken with the food that we used to take daily. For supper, we had nothing to eat for a few months, until the Red Cross came. We slept on the cement. We were so many people that it was necessary for us to sleep one upon the other. We were more than one thousand and five hundred people in the camp, but I was the youngest. I fought just like one of those men.

I hope that the American youths of my age do not suffer as I did, or preferably do not suffer at all. Be happy, you American youths, because the leaders of your country really tried to protect you. About my country, I would never say that our leaders did not try to protect us. They did, and as far as Greece is concerned, they gave the best example in history during World War II.

After that sacrifice, I came out fine. I am thankful just because I am alive. I am thankful because I came to America, and I forgot about the terrible event in my life. I hope to get a chance for a good life in this country, which is blessed by God.

THE CONQUERORS AND I

[Editor's Note: This was originally published in Spring 1950 in the Moline High School literary magazine, *The Imp*.]

I was a very young man when it was my fate to be under terrible barbarian rulers, the conquerors of Greece during the years 1941-1945. The conquerors of Greece were two great tyrants, Mussolini and Hitler.

In 1941, all the people of Greece were suffering from the greatest and most terrible depression that Greece ever had. I can never forget that year. On April 13, 1941, just ten days before Easter, I remember, I left my sweet mother, my brothers, my sister, my relatives, my friends, and my beautiful town, and went to Thessaly, a state in Greece. My grandfather was there. He was really glad to see me. So was my grandmother.

My grandfather there owns many acres of land, and also a lot of animals. Oh, yes, I had a good time for about twenty-five days. When I awoke on May 6, the morning was beautiful. As I walked down to the village, I heard the birds singing. The water of the river was very quiet, beautiful flowers ornamented the earth, and the trees were all flowered and green. Oh, it was such a beautiful day! As I walked down the riverside, I found a beautiful place to lie down and enjoy nature.

The sun came out. Now with the sun shining, the birds singing, and the flowers blooming, I was happy as a boy in childhood, and I started to sing. Oh, I can't tell all the details of that morning. I was feeling so good and so glad that I had joined my grandparents and that I was having such a good time, and could enjoy so much good food.

While I spent two hours among the beautiful flowers, I began to think about my mother, brothers, sister, and my town. As I was thinking, I heard something. Quickly, I got up to see what it was. At that time, an Italian soldier saw me. He told me to halt. "Yes, sir, I have halted," I answered. Then he came near me and looked in my pockets to see if I had anything. He didn't find anything except my handkerchief, and some candy that my grandmother had given me the day before. He slapped me. I said, "Why did you do that? What did I do to you?" He did not answer me. I got really mad, but what could I do? I just remained. Then he took me to the camp.

An Italian officer came in front of me and asked, "What do you know about the Greek Revolutionary Army?" I was greatly frightened. But even though I was only twelve years old, I felt great pride in my country, and would have liked to answer, "If I were older, I would enjoy fighting against you barbarians." But I said nothing because I realized I was in his power. I also realized his cruelty and injustice. He said, "You Hellenes think we are barbarians and good for nothing to rule. And much more than that, which is unthinkable to tell." I said nothing because I realized it would not be wise. But I would have liked to say, "You, the killers, the tyrants, have spoiled almost everything in our country. We are powerless, but we are proud and will some day rise." They then put me into the train and sent me to the concentration camp of Larissa. There were about one thousand five hundred people under barbarian rule.

On May 10, I arrived at the concentration camp. I saw the big buildings, and thought it would be good to live in such beautiful buildings. But when I came into the camp and saw how they lived there, it was really a tragedy. There, people, without food, without many things, without beds, were sleeping on the cement floors. Such fate was not only my fate, but also that of the older men. I went to the camp without coat and shoes. Every day they used us as slaves to work in cement factories and airports. Yes, proudly I worked, even if I was hungry and thirsty. For food, they gave us only fifteen ounces of soup and a little bread. We all paid a terrible price.

Later, the Red Cross took care and sent us beds, covers, medicine, more food, and other supplies that we should have. Soon, the slave Greeks from that camp changed. We became better looking and stronger. In each cabin, we had a captain who would take care of as many things as he could. At the same time, the Red Cross gave us a doctor, and one of the buildings was used as a hospital.

Next came the terrible day of August 19, 1941. The Italians took a hundred and six young Greek men out to the camp for killing. In that group, I was called too. We followed the orders of the barbarian rulers as they directed us into the killing camp, called Cournavo. Two German officers came along on their motorcycles to save me, just because I was young.

They returned me to the camp where, from my terror, worry, and other suffering, I became sick. In the meantime, my grandparents did not know anything about what had happened, and looked a long time to find me. At last, they found me by asking the Red Cross.

After six months and seven days, two representatives of the U.S.A., members of the Red Cross in Greece, talked to the conquerors, who let me out. The Red Cross sent me in a car to my grandfather in the city of Domoco. My grandfather sent me back to my town, Hohlia. The people of my town called at my house to visit me. They brought flowers of many kinds.

LIFE IN AMERICA

THANKS TO MY NEW COUNTRY

I was born in a very small town, Hohlia, in Greece. [Editor's Note: John lived for much of his childhood in Hohlia, but he was actually born in the near-by town of Petralona.]

Frequently, I went to the large city of Domoco, in the state of Thessaly. There, I helped my grandfather, George, who was a farmer. He had many sheep, goats, horses, and cows. During World War II, I was there while the Greeks suffered terribly.

On February 5, 1947, I arrived from Greece, and came to this happy America. I started at the age of 18 to go to school at Calvin Coolidge Junior High School. In December 1948, I started Moline High School, where I have had a happy school life. I feel very happy in this country of the United States of America.

I want to thank from the depth of my heart the schools, teachers, students, and all the people of Moline. I will never forget the librarians and teachers of CCJHS. In addition, I will never forget Miss L. Johnson, my history teacher, or Miss M. Hendee, my English teacher. They will stay in my heart forever. Thank you.

Seeing New and Strange Things

When I first came from my country, I traveled straight to New York. I arrived at night, and I could not see well. When we entered New York harbor, all the people came to the top floor of the ship to see the glorious American Statue of Liberty. When I first came to America, I did not know much about the Statue of Liberty. Now I have learned that the Statue of Liberty is the point of freedom, liberty, education, and democracy.

New York is a very famed city with her great modern architecture. Her tall buildings are renowned all over the world. These modern buildings hold more than a thousand people. When I first saw them, I thought it was one of my dreams; I thought I was sleeping and dreamed up the great buildings of New York. Some of them are thousands of yards in the earth. So much did I like New York and its buildings that I hope to go again someday.

Next, I came to Davenport, Iowa, with her beautiful and aristocratic Blackhawk Hotel. The hotel is very notable for its Golden Hall, where most of the wealthy people in the Quad Cities hold their wedding receptions. In my three years in this city, most of the weddings I went to were at the Blackhawk Hotel. Why do people like that hotel better than any other? We have a number of good hotels in Davenport, but the Blackhawk Hotel gives better service than any other hotel, as some people say.

Moline, East Moline, and Silvis are the next three cities that I saw. Moline is the city in which I have lived for three years now. Attending its schools is enjoyable. I think Moline is one of the best cities in the Quad Cities. It has a number of beautiful things. For example, Fifth Avenue, which is the main avenue in Moline, is ornamented on each side by nice buildings. This is the first city I enjoyed in the United States since I came from Greece.

About East Moline, I know little. I have never looked closely at that town, because I always travel by bus through it on my way to Silvis. It looks only a little different from Moline. It has a very nice high school, from how it looks outside. Also, it has a good palladium to play football.

Silvis is a little town, but I like it very much. During the summer, I go out to the farms of Silvis. I think it has a very good nature. Fresh air, coolness, animals in the farm, and many other things fill me with so much pleasure.

THE STREETS OF MOLINE (ILLINOIS)

For the past three years, I have lived in the city of Moline without learning the city streets well. That is not because I am not interested in the city. My daily work does not give me the opportunity to go around the city, and to learn every single corner, the beauty of the parks, or other public places that make people feel enthusiastic and pleased.

The streets that I pass every day are 19th Street and Fifth Avenue. During a parade such as a school celebration, hundreds of people are in Fifth Avenue waiting to see the parade. You hear many loud sounds of women and men speaking during the day's celebration.

Throughout the city streets are many foreigners, who know little of the English language. Instead, they use their native languages. Such people speak Mexican, Greek, Swedish, and other kinds of languages.

The famous Fifth Avenue is always clean and nice. Even after living in the city of Moline for almost three years, as yet I have not seen any banana peels thrown into the streets. The city itself puts containers in every corner for discarding unneeded things. So the people should listen to the voice of the city, and keep their streets clean of banana peels.

Women with three or more babies walk in the streets. I saw a woman and man with four babies, but I do not know, of course, if all of them were theirs. The babies seemed to be of different ages. Although one of them was able to walk, the other three were not. One of them was in the baby carriage, two others were in the lap of the woman, and the other one was in the lap of the man. All of them were good-looking and healthy. They seemed to be happy. The couple who seemed to be their parents looked very proud.

Dogs walk on the street with short and long tails. They sniff and walk around people.

The newsboys who sell newspapers in the street try smartly to sell newspapers. My younger brother, an eleven-year old boy, sells newspapers for two companies throughout the streets of Moline. One is the Daily Times, and the other is the Chicago News. He is very much interested to be a salesman.

MY EXPERIENCE IN A GROCERY STORE

I have now worked two and a half years in the grocery store, and had the opportunity to enjoy each department systematically. At first, I tried the warehouse. Later, I worked in the fruit department, and then in the meat department. Now, I work everywhere in the store.

When longtime customers come into the store, they usually know where each thing is placed. Other customers who are new have no idea of the placement of each individual thing. You have to take the customer, and direct him to the place where the thing that he asks for is located.

Fruit Department

In the fruit department, there is usually much work to attend to. When the truck man brings the fruits, the checker must be careful. The checker checks the incoming fruits. He opens the boxes to see if the fruits are in the condition in which they should be. Some things are rotten and will have to be thrown away the next day. The fruits are put in the cooler to keep them fresh. Usually, the tomatoes do not go in the cooler because they do not have to be kept cool. If the tomatoes are green and you want to ripen them as early as possible, first take a few newspapers and wet them with water, and then put them on top of the tomatoes. Let them stay like that for about 24 hours, then the tomatoes will be ready for sale.

It is not only the tomatoes that must be checked. In the summer, the peaches, plums, pears, and more things must be checked every day. In the winter, the checker must keep things the right way. The checker has to check the cooler for oranges and grapes. In the spring, when the new fruits come to us, we usually like them better than the old. But the fruit salesman must sell the old first, and then the new. If he does not sell them, his accounts will decrease.

Meat Department

The meat department is harder to work in than the fruit department. Much more attention is needed. The butcher must always keep his eyes on the freezers, because sometimes the electricity is cut off, and the meat is thoroughly spoiled. The meat checkers must know how to check calves. Each calf must have a stamp from the United States animal health department. In addition, the butcher must know how to clean the chickens.

THE MOLINE PUBLIC LIBRARY

I am glad for this opportunity to describe my experience with the Moline Public Library. It has given me great service and help. When I came to Moline three years ago, I had no knowledge of the English language, and no experience with using a library. The librarians were good to help me with any question I asked them. They especially surprised me with their sweet character. They really loved to help a foreign boy to learn, and to be a good American citizen. They brought several books from other libraries, in Rock Island and Davenport. The books were written in Greek and were translated into English so that I could get the ideas both ways. I will long remember the city of Moline and its people of good character.

Moline Public Library was built in 1903, just a little after Moline formed a city government. Andrew Carnegie gave a donation of 40 thousand dollars for the building. Others also gave donations for the building, including the first mayor of Moline, whose name I can't remember. He also gave a bunch of money for establishing a house in the spirit of education.

IN DEFENSE OF SPEAKING ONE'S NATIVE TONGUE IN AMERICA

In this great America, where we are assembled in a democratic way, and enjoy the freedom of Washington, most people are happy. In certain cases, however, some people are not. Why? As far as America is concerned, it is full of foreign people who come to America without knowledge of English. The foreigners try to learn. Some American people fool the poor foreigners. As some Greek people tell me, when they came to America 40 years ago, they were afraid to say that they were Greek. That is not a complaint only among the Greeks, but among many other nationalities. Now, it is different, and my own experience should be different. The Americans should be taught to stop their foolishness against the foreigners, no matter what kind of nationality they have.

In a book written a hundred years ago, the author explains that Americans have changed. The Americans not only stopped fooling the poor foreigners, but also started to help them to be good American citizens. That is how you could help me to learn many things I don't know.

Although you help the foreign people as much as you can, you also tell them not to speak their own language, and to speak English. Why? I don't understand why they should.

My own language is Hellenic, the Mother of the world's languages. I am a Hellene. I came from Hellas two years ago to enjoy America. I see that most colleges in America teach the ancient Hellenic language incorrectly [i.e., not according to Modern Greek pronunciation]. In colleges in Hellas, even at the University of Athens, the oldest one, they do not teach it that way. I have been there, and I know.

In my country Hellas, there are many Americans today. There is a lovely friendship between the Hellenic people and Americans. The American people overseas learn the Hellenic language, but they still speak their own (English). The Hellenic people never tell them to forget English. Most of the Hellenic people meet with the United States Army or its people who are over there and help them to learn the Hellenic language. At the same time, the United States people help the Hellenics to learn English, which is very interesting.

THE SUCCESS OF GREEK IMMIGRANTS

Up to this time, Americans have regarded the Greeks as an inferior race, although they are smart in business and making good money. Their faults have been magnified. If any non-English speaking foreigner of dark complexion is accused of a grave offense, Americans are too ready to surmise that he is of Greek origin, and so it is published by the American press under glaring headlines.

And yet, in this country where the libraries are filled with works of Greek literature, science, and art, one we should expect a better appreciation of the descendants of the world's greatest artists and philosophers.

In the days of old, wherever Greeks settled, they imparted their knowledge to those with whom they came in contact. So in our present days, wherever Greeks choose an abode, they are inferior to none. They have been respected and esteemed. They have done honor to those countries in which they lived, and in which we the Greeks of today live.

There is not a country in the world where the Greeks have not been distinguished among all the other nationalities. All over the world, Greeks are professors, army and navy officers, and hold other high offices. Greeks in London, Manchester, and Liverpool are wealthy. Quite a few of them have been honored with titles. Greeks in Paris and Marseilles occupy prominent professorships, and constitute the best class of society. In Russia, they have reached the highest offices, as mayors of the largest cities, and as ministers. In Romania, the rulers of that country were Greeks while yet under Turkish dominion. Even some of the most prominent statesmen of today are of Greek descent. In Egypt, Greeks control commerce. Likewise in Turkey, they have had supremacy over all other races without exception.

Many of the Greeks that have acquired renown in foreign lands started their careers much like the poor, uneducated immigrants of this country. Rapidly, they rose to the summit of distinction. The secret of the

Greeks' success lies not only in our cleverness and business ability, but in our deep appreciation for the people among whom our fathers lived and we live. It is this appreciation that is lacking on the part of the American people. In spite of that, the Greeks of this country have pushed our way eagerly to attain the goal of success. We remain faithful to our tradition to be inferior to none. We follow in the footsteps of our fellow countrymen all over the globe.

It should be remembered that Greek immigration started systematically less than 50 years ago. The great majority of immigrants have come only within the last 20 years. Without education, without business experience, without knowledge of the English language, without friends, Greeks have struggled against every obstacle. Thousands of these ignorant and poor immigrants are now well-to-do, and contribute to the wealth of this country. Thousands, likewise, are in the colleges and universities throughout the country, in pursuit of higher studies. Almost all of them are distinguished among their classmates, attracting the particular attention and praise of their professors.

As workers, we the Greeks offer our bodily strength and often our lives. As soldiers, we are an example of fearlessness and bravery. As businessmen, we prove our ingenuity and our instinctive shrewdness. We have been the pioneers in the confectionery, fruit, and restaurant businesses throughout the country. There is not a city or town in the United States where one will not find Greek confectionery stores or restaurants. The greatest manufacturers of Turkish and Egyptian cigarettes in America are Greeks. A few of them who started with neither money nor education have become millionaires in a very short time.

As men of letters, we the Greeks are distinguished for our brightness of mind and our inborn refinement. As artists we are inspired by our creative genius, that splendid inheritance from our forefathers. It is not a rare thing to discover a modern Phidias in a boot-black parlor. [Editor's Note: John's teacher commented, "I found one, a fine student and cultured Greek, in a shoe shine parlor in Moline. This surprised me much. But this was before I knew Greeks."] Many Greeks carry off the prize in artistic contests from among scores who are fighting for the laurel.

NOT THE SCHOOL, BUT THE STUDENTS

[Editor's Note: This was originally published in the Moline High School newspaper.]

I came to the United States just a little more than two years ago, and have attended the public schools of Moline. When I first came, I couldn't speak English at all. Now, I have improved my language with the help of my fellow students and my spiritual teachers. I wish to express my appreciation and thanks to God who gave me the good luck and joy to attend the Moline High School, from which I will graduate next June.

My first assignment to write for the school paper has the title, "Not the School, but the Students." Some days ago, I looked in a big dictionary to find a better way of expressing the meaning of school. School is not the building itself, but the cooperation of a group of people working together to learn something better.

It was interesting to me to see the differences between the schools of the United States and those of Greece. One great difference is that the students here are full of happiness and fun. Still, a student who comes to school does not come to the big and beautiful buildings for a rest, or to sit down and have a good time. A student comes to study under his teacher. The chair of your classroom is very comfortable, but your eyes and your head get tired. Yet, they won't hurt very much after we graduate. We will use the experience that we are getting now, although it seems so hard to us today, to make our lives easier tomorrow.

This year, I had the opportunity to be elected to the Student Congress. In Greece, we do not have student elections. Instead, the principal of the school appoints a student from the highest class to represent the school, similar to a king in a monarchical democracy. In each country, the student government is patterned after the government of the country.

PHILOSOPHY OF LIFE

GREAT POWER IN WORDS

Are you ill, poor, a failure or discouraged? Do you really want to get well? Reach? Most of the people think they want to, but they don't do anything about it.

Are you one of those people? Do you expect your teacher to be a magician? Do you expect that teacher whom you face at this moment to cure you? If you do, you are wasting your time, friends, for the cure comes from within and not from any other place. Unless you assume your share of responsibility, you cannot reap.

Some of us are willing to hold on to our ailments, unconscious fixations, and phobias. We magnify symptoms to preposterous proportions. Jesus, after curing the afflicted, directed that, "He goes and tells no man." He wanted to make sure that dwelling on the ailment or cure would not reinforce the fixations of the unconscious. There was always the fear that some individual would reconvince the sufferer that he was, or still is, ill.

A real example of the power of words happened in my town. A high ranking State police official, who was from the same town as I, was stricken in both legs with paralysis. Every method of medicine and aid was tried. At last, the afflicted one tried a chiropractic procedure, and his limbs were restored. Some months later, a dinner was given by his friends in his honor to celebrate his recovery.

A detective walked over to him as the party became lively and said, "Sure, John, they were only kidding you, there was nothing the matter with you. It was in your mind, that's all." From that ill moment, this man never walked again. As my friends from Greece inform me, he is crippled to this day.

Be careful what you say. Remember, there is great power in words, more power than in a shotgun. Remember how mere words sent many innocent men to the gallows. Words have destroyed many homes, fortunes, and worst of all, the character of many good men and women. Be careful in the use of words and thoughts, for thoughts are things, and words do crystallize.

Remember, you will not be in school for all of your life. As you do not have the opportunity to extend school, the most joyful time of your life, try to remember the most important things that you learn today for the rest of your life.

Remember to use nice words among your friends, family, co-workers, and especially to your own children tomorrow, for your children will be whatever your words are, good or bad. As the Lord said, "Be it done to you as your faith."

And all that means is, if you want to be well or rich, you will; if you want to be ill, you will. Whatever you want to be, you will be.

WE ALL LOVE LIFE

September 6, 1949

Dear Reader:

Recently, I read in the *Reader's Digest* a short story that attracted my attention greatly. In this short story, a preacher asked all those in his congregation who wanted to go to heaven to stand. Everybody stood except one man. The preacher then told everybody to sit down. He asked all those who wanted to go to the "other place" to stand. This time, everyone remained seated. The preacher looked down his glasses, pointed a finger at the man who had remained seated both times, and demanded an explanation. The man answered very simply, "I like it here where I am!" Well, I guess that all of us love life.

The *Herald-American* magazine carried the following moral statement: "We all love Life. Do not squander time. There will be time enough to sleep in the grave." This line really made me pause and meditate. How true is this simple sentence. We always think that we will live forever. We keep looking to the better days to come, when all along time is slipping by. To this, I have something more to add. If you love living, do not spend your hours and minutes foolishly. Enjoy every minute of every day. When we are healthy, then life is really beautiful. All of us have the tendency to plan and dream about that glorious day in the future when all will be just the way we want it. In the meantime, the hours are slipping away and that day, sad to relate, hardly ever comes just as we want it to. So enjoy this day.

The man who did not want to go to heaven or Hades expressed a simple truth. None of us wants to leave this earth. We cannot change the laws of nature. The next best thing is to live each day to the fullest. We warp our vision by things that do not matter and we fill our minds with petty things that obscure our clear thinking. Truly, there is so much that is beautiful right here on earth. We humans are always looking for something when we have everything right before our eyes.

Today, it is a beautiful day. The sky is robin's egg blue. The clouds could be a painting of Moline on canvas. The golden season of the earth, and the bright sunshine, add zest to living. There is human peacefulness during this Sunday, and all the people are relaxing. Even the children are dressed in their best, and seem to be subdued. Isn't it a wonderful feeling to be alive on such a day?

The cares that loom so large before your eyes now will fade into forgetfulness a few months from now. You will wonder what you ever had to worry about. The aches and pains that annoy you now will go away. You will not remember what troubled you.

So why not push the troublesome things out of our minds and hearts? Look at the wonderful things that God has placed on earth for our sheer pleasure. Enjoy this day and every day. There will be time enough to sleep when the time comes to leave this life.

PHILOSOPHY

1. The fire of love is the only fire that nobody can insure himself against.

2. Love is the only game that can be played by two players and lost by both.

3. It is much better to fall in love with somebody, and to lose one's sweetheart, than never to love at all. At least this love will benefit the flower seller, the sweet seller, the businessman, and sometimes the lawyer.

4. Do good deeds on earth, and then forget them.

5. Pray to God so that He helps you in a moment of danger, but you must move for Him to help you.

6. A good soldier fears only God and dishonor.

7. A virgin woman must always stay far from men.

8. Communists do not believe in God because they expect God to give them food without any work

9. Democracy always gets ahead because it works hard.

ABRAHAM LINCOLN

To his memory on his birthday. Freedom illuminated Abraham Lincoln.

On February 12, 1809, 141 years ago, in a tiny log cabin in Kentucky, a child was born who was to become a symbol of liberty and freedom for the oppressed throughout the world. This child was Abraham Lincoln. According to a biography of Lincoln in our public library, Lincoln did not greatly impress his teachers or acquaintances during his early years other than with his love for books. In those days, books were at a premium in the rural areas of the Middle West. The few he was able to procure he read many, many times.

Thomas Lincoln, his father, was a poor farmer who placed muscular prowess above mental abilities. He did not sympathize with his son's yearning for knowledge. His stepmother, however, became his willing ally. She taught him, and shielded him from his father's occupation.

In Lincoln's autobiography, I also found a very wise statement that gave me the idea to write my theme. On a flatboat trip to New Orleans, he had his first glimpse of Negro slaves being auctioned as cattle. His emotions and sympathy were aroused and he made the statement, "If I ever get a chance to hit slavery, I'll hit it hard." Little did he or his friends realize just what opportunities were to be his to do that great thing.

Springfield, Illinois is proud of Abraham Lincoln. It is really his home. The only house he ever owned was located in that city, and is still standing. That is the home where he married and where his children were born. That is the city along whose streets he was a familiar figure and whose homes and shops his voice echoed as he told timely jokes and passed the time of day. That is the city in which he is buried and to whose tomb thousands of people come each year to pay their respects and to place a wreath in his memory. These people come from all parts of the world, wherever freedom-loving people live.

In 1945, Springfield was honored by a visit by the renowned Greek admiral and former commander-in-chief of the Greek Navy, Alexander Sakelariou of Athens, Greece. The next year, the famous and heroic General Papagos of the Greek Army visited Springfield. Both men placed wreaths on the tomb in behalf of the people of Greece who are ever striving to keep their freedom.

PATRIOTISM

GREEK HEROISM

We who are assembled today in this country, the United States of America, are loyal friends of democracy. We are bound together by common interests and ties, including: love for the United States of America and Greece; admiration of Greek culture, talent, and courage; a desire to promote friendly relations in the united world of today; and determination to do all that is possible and proper to aid Greece to maintain her Independence, and to become again a self-supporting and prosperous state that is free to play a role in the world worthy of her great heritage. Such common ties and interests cannot but create among us an atmosphere of intimacy that encourages the free interchange of thought.

It has been almost 3,000 years since there began to glow in Greece the sparks of a new culture, based in democracy, tolerance, and respect for the dignity and rights of men. These sparks gradually developed into a flame of such brightness that it penetrated all the recesses of the then known world. During the vicissitudes of the intervening centuries, the light emanating from Greece was threatened. Nevertheless, it has never been completely smothered. Since Greek liberation about a century and a quarter ago, it has been again gaining in brightness. Even during the centuries when Greece was deprived of her political independence, the Greek people, by their stubborn adherence to the principles of democracy, and by their sustained struggle for freedom, continued to set up an inspiring example for liberty loving people everywhere. It would be a tragedy if in our generation the flame that has survived through the milleniums should be finally extinguished.

I wrote my poems to help the people of America understand the life and heroism of the Greek people. (I was able to write these poems because I worked hard with my old Greek dictionary at the Moline Public Library, everyday after school for almost three months.) At any time and in any place, the Greek people are ready to survive, but also to give their life for the government that rules them. The student of these poems will understand the meaning of love, country, nationality, and freedom. We, the men of the United World of today, must know and understand with courage the meaning of these four concepts. Have a good look at this, and think about it carefully, because there is a long way for humans being to go!

GREECE FOR POLITICAL AND TERRITORIAL INDEPENDENCE

For over three years, Greece has fought to defend her political and territorial independence. In the last six months, a stage has been reached in which it may reasonably be said that the internal strife has entered the final phase. The anxieties of the Greek leaders in Greece are now of a wider scope and of the same nature as the preoccupations of the western world in its efforts for peace. The blows that the regular army, now much bigger and better equipped, has dealt against the fortified rebel strongholds in the inaccessible Granor Massif, in the district of Vitsi, near Florina, and in the Volvi mountains of Macedonia in eastern Greece, are so decisive that, after the completion of the campaign in Peloponessos and Roumelis, it should be possible to reach a final conclusion to the trouble in Greece before Russia gets in.

This conviction prevails both among Greek military experts and among the fellows of the American military mission. After the complete mopping-up by the regular army and gendarmerie forces, if the rebel leaders come to the conclusion that further resistance is useless and try to secure a prospect of normal political development for the communist parties of foreign countries, the rebel nests should disappear automatically. In fact, it seems that the rebels have suffered very heavy blows, which have created in the Greek public opinion a great resolve that will no longer tolerate the half-measures of political solutions.

This was the atmosphere in which the rebels' "peace feelers" were received. Not only the government, but also the man in the street, who only a few months ago would perhaps have been disposed to lend a willing ear to proposals of some kind of political compromise with the rebels (as the military operations did not open any horizons of more drastic solutions), today simply dismiss the proposals, which have the additional disadvantage of following after Moscow's dictatorship. Greece never reverted to dictatorship from democracy for many centuries, not since Pericles of Athens lighted the torch of Democracy, giving freedom to all people in Greece.

The United States takes in hand today the leadership of Democracy, which Pericles showed to the Athenian people three thousand years ago. When the mother of Democracy called for help, the United States came, for she always helps countries that help themselves.

THE RUSSIAN BEAR

The Russian bear is growling just a little bit louder of late. And it's definitely on the move. On the prowl would be a more suitable expression. While we in the United States are determined to live and let live, the Russian Bear casts a greedy eye toward the United States, a coveted land indeed. Were we to survey the Russian airfields and military concentrations just across the Bering Sea from Alaska, we might readily surmise that Russia is planning to attack America.

It so happens that the Soviets do not welcome our inspections. The real reason that Stalin, Molotov, and the Politburo refused Bernard M. Baruch's plan for bomb production is that it would mean open inspection of bomb making. From history we learn that the Reds have always dreaded inspection, so it's hardly likely that they will welcome it now.

Yet, on a particularly sunny day it is possible without spying to note the concentration of Russian defenses on the western side of the Bering Sea. Russia's heavy fortifications of her territory close to Alaska may indicate her intention to attack Alaska. She still has a great many Americans wondering.

Although we ourselves in the United States have considerable air forces in Alaska, we certainly don't intend to attack Russian Siberia. On the other hand, we know too well that Russia is the only power capable of undertaking a war against the United States. We positively don't want war. But does Russia? Only Russia knows the answer to this enigma. We in America look for the answer for our own sake, as well for the sake of world peace.

All we know is that the Big Bear has emerged from its hibernation and is raring to go. After eons of inertia, Russia is suddenly filled with ardor in behalf of communism. The Russians idolize Marx, Engels, and Lenin. Meanwhile, the Reds persist in expanding their economic ambitions on victims who welcome them.

We know that the President Truman Plan for aiding Europe has made great demands on us, and that the demands will tend to increase. But are we to abandon our friends who think and hope the way we do, only because our pockets are being drained? I think America should continue to help those European countries that are trying to help themselves. Wherever possible, we must efface discontent, which makes the underdog willing bait to the communistic missionaries.

THE ATOMIC BOMB

I. Ancient History

Five hundred years before Christ, atomic theory was discovered in Greece. The philosopher Leuccipus, with his best pupil Democritus, thought it wise to discover atomic energy. Atomic theory was actually hypothesized about a century and a quarter before Democritus by Thalas, another philosopher of Athens. Thalas tried through speeches to interest Athenians in atomic theory. He died at an early age, and did not have the opportunity to work on his theory. Later, Leucippus and Democritus worked on carrying out Thalas's thought.

As Democritus said, he wanted to discover the atomic bomb to protect democracy in Greece. The philosophers did not work to discover atomic theory for bombs only, but also for many other scientific purposes. There are many medicines today that are made from atoms.

II. Nature

The philosophers imagined two types of atomic bombs. The first type is the Anaremones, which was prepared with air. For example, in physics, one can take a can, fill it with air, close it well, and then put it in the fire. If one abuses it, the can will blow. Thus, it was the first natural way to think about making an atomic bomb.

The second type is the Eracliton, which is the mix of air and water together. Leucippus and Democritus made their first atomic bomb with air and water. It could not do any harm in war. Later, when Aristotle worked to make an atomic bomb, he increased the atomic energy. He added air with salt. He got salt by using seawater instead of fresh water.

III. High Ideals

Many people tried to discover an atomic bomb to destroy the world. Another great philosopher worked on the dynamitical fire, and made a geometrical theory. About three hundred years later, the Roman poet Lucretius wrote the greatest philosophical poem about the atomic bomb. But nobody could discover more than the Greek philosophers did.

Atomic theory was spread all over the world, and factories were made for it. Atomic theory went first to Russia, later to Germany, Italy, and other countries, but they remained without a bomb. In the late 1800's, Joseph John Thomson, a Britishman, discovered electrons that were one of the most important discoveries to add to the atomic bomb. Robert Boyle of America, and G. Gannow of Russia, discovered how to use alpha and beta particles and gamma and x-rays to light an atomic bomb. They still had not discovered an atomic bomb.

IV. War and Tragedy

On July 16, 1945, the United States Army Corps completed the atomic bomb at the District of Columbia. It was used during the last war for world peace. The atomic bomb caused a tragedy when President Truman first ordered its use. American heroes used the first atomic bomb in Japan. The second bomb was used at Nagasaki. The tragedy of this bomb is that most people died. The bomb was noisy, dirty, and smelly.

V. Effectiveness

Today, there are 49 types of atomic bombs, but three are the most destructive. The most destructive is the uranium bomb, which contains the most weight. The second one is the hydrogen bomb, which does not have the same weight. The third one is the so-called atomic bomb. It is also a destructive machine like the uranium bomb.

VI. Patriotism

The atomic bomb was discovered because of patriotism. When Leucippus tried to make a bomb, he wanted to protect democracy in Greece. So it is today that the United States taking leadership of democracy makes necessary the production of atomic bombs to protect the world's democracy and peace from communist hordes.

VII. Philosophy

The modern philosophers relate very closely with those scientific philosophers of the ancient ages. It took 28 centuries of work to make the atomic machine, which was completed in 1945. As yet, it has not been as destructive as it might well be if it is used during the next war, if we are going to have one.

POEMS

PHILOSOPHY

PHILOSOPHY*

I saw the master of those I know
Amid the philosophic family,
By all admired, and by all revered.
There too, I saw Plato and Socrates
Who stand first, and behind them all the others.

GOD'S BLESSING*

Scatter your blessing,
Not only in this land,
But all over the world, from acre to acre.
God, make the nations see
That people must be brothers,
To form one family
All over the world.

[Editor's Note: Poems with asterisks were translated from the Greek.]

GOD*

God! Hymns praise your glory night and day.
With flowers you cover the earth, with stars the heavens.
The people of the earth praise you at all times.
A thousand varieties of languages praise you in symphony.
You count the uncounted.
You order the unordered.
You think the unthought.
You know the unknown.
God, the light is your body,
The sun is your company,
And the thunderbolt is your voice.
Infinite is your great stature,
And the century is one of your minutes.
Your finger is able,
Like a crowbar, to move the earth,
And the palm of your hand
Can shut the oceans.
Only your spirit can blow out
The light of the stars,
And only your nod can close
The heaven from the earth.

THE RED RIVER

Came the river noisily,
With red, dirty water,
Sweeping the plains, meadows, and vineyards,
Breaking trees and fences,
Taking away animals and souls.
We hear mournful voices of church bells.
The skies are dark and full of thunder.
Here am I,
And my heart totters.
The thread of music and lyricism
Will be cut.
But it will not be cut.
Lord, turn your eye to see
The earth's violence.
Turn your eye to see
Terrors, voices, roarings of the earth.
Many souls in the river
Are tottering like reeds
Bent by the angry air.
Lord, take this violence out to the ocean.
Turn your great affection
To silence the violence,
To make the rivers into clean, white water.
Now is the hour for bells of light, sweet voices.

MY PHILOSOPHY

Years and years I spent
Thinking through so many nights.
Through all my youth I worked,
And, little by little, I learned.
I learned the story of Socrates,
I learned the law of Lykurgus.
I learned of the bravery of Alexander the Great,
And the simple grandeur of George Washington.
These last two stars of the world
Are quite enough for me to know.
They, who glorified their sphere
With liberty, union, and freedom.
I learned what philosophy means.
Philosophy means love,
To love your parents, your brothers,
Your teachers, and your professors.

YOU'LL BE HAPPY TO LIVE

Once I was told,
I don't love life,
Living as I live.
After a few minutes,
I changed my thinking,
And it became more logical.
Think of a life, in which
You work only so hard.
Enjoy the rest
Of the day's living hour.
Enjoy the dance.
Enjoy the play.
Enjoy everything,
And you will be happy to live.

ON MY BIRTHDAY

Other people cheerfully
Celebrate the day
Because they want life.
Life is never called a continuous pain.
Yet, my heart feels much heavier.
My cries are more earnest.
How not to cry! I lost one of my years,
Completely without desire to see anyone.
Every year, my face only wrinkles,
And time leaves its mark.
How not to cry! I lived without living.
I'll die before I know life.
I ask myself a question,
Why does man
Come free into the world,
And die a slave?
It's not folly to me
To go deeply into my heart.
That is where I hide my hurts.
Let my secret die with me.

PATRIOTISM

WAR SONG*

The army knife is in the palm again.
Blood, like a river, let it spill!
The Italians and the Germans call us
Thessalians, Epirotes, Macedonians, and Thracians.
Mount Athos in blood, and Mount Pindos like a snake.
Bring to them on the noisy voiced tongue
Instead of flint sown in the earth
Only one sparks, only one they await.
Children of Greece, become sparks.
Leaders, become saviours of the race.

ODE TO MY TOWN, KARPENISI*

Bloody, and still hot
From the fire,
The glorious earth rises,
And conquers our terrible slavery.
Greetings, Karpenisi. Centuries of blood
Have defended your sweet liberty.
Glorious graves and luminous contests
Decorate you with light.
You sow your streets with holy tears,
Your mother is a hidden pulse.
And the entrails deprive her throne
As a pledge, into your heavenly light.

ODE TO THE GREEKS*

Mussolini, a eunuch's nursling,
Wild tiger, and dreadful beast,
Sips Greek blood rabidly,
The blood of men, old people, and children.
He orders death to the immortal Greeks.
He sends his people everywhere with guns.
But his army is the flock of a slave,
While our army is an army of heroes.
He tries to use his armed forces,
Trenches, bulwarks, high fortresses,
And fire from infinite cannons,
But he fails to conquer the bravery of the Greeks.
These new contests of Thermopylae,
Against this new Persia,
Ensure the immortality
Of the courageous, Greek people.

WAR SONG (II)*

I'm sorry that my prodigal heart scattered
So many of my feelings, here and there, in passing.
Those who have them now do not treasure them.
I should have watered them with tears of joy in the immortal ground.
Here, where I would have eternal glory,
To ornament Mount Velouchi with fir trees and laurel.
Ah! If I could also ornament it with a poor flower,
So much I do love you, even if I don't know it.
I make to you an oath before God, in the foreign lands that I wander,
That not an hour will pass when I will not think of you.
Karpenession, the land of zeal,
Please don't forget this.
Anyone in the world who loves, must also be loved,
And that memory lessens the pain.
The nightingale sings with joy sometimes,
Despite his dark slavery in the beautiful Velouchi.
Fate is written with a cursed logic.
Curse you, exile, who ate my youth,
Not letting me enjoy the company of young men
Who are full of vigor,
And full of heart.
I leave you, Karpenission, with pain I leave you.
I go to my dark slavery,
But I leave my poor heart with you.
Be well, golden eagle, be well, my town.
You may forget me, but not my heart.

GREEK & ITALIAN WAR IN ALBANIA (1941): A LITTLE DRAMA*

Greece:
Hold on here, you Italians, hold on and tell me,
What do you want near me, as if I belonged to you?
I am a Greek land, and I won't live as a slave.
Country of Alexander and Aristotle,
The place from where
They gave light to all the world,
And still enlighten it.
Italy:
I want to take your beauty.
You have mountains like forts,
And hills with cool water.
You have many beautiful things.
I will have you work, as my slave, for my children.
Greece:
I'll never be slave to you, you terrible race.
Inside me boils fast the blood of my mother
If a little blood spills, and makes the earth red,
You will see that this earth will shoot fire that will burn you.
I was a slave at one time because it was my fate.
Still, the Turks respected me, and I saved my honor,
My religion, and even my life.
And if God wants, I'll live happily with victory forever.
You are different than me.
Go away, Italians, and mind your own business.
Italy:
Come, golden, Greek girl, become Italian.
Come and marry an Italian, who wears his high, fur hat.
Because it is desolate, dark, and black,
You have no close relatives near you,
And you have no one trustworthy
To turn to and tell your pain.
Greece:
You know that I won't marry you. I'll live free.

Rather than take an Italian husband, I'll go to my mother.
But don't think I have no relatives.
I have the Roumelis as my sister, and the Morea as my brother,
And the Islands as my beloved brothers, and Crete as my beloved sister.
Woe to you when they come here to defend me.

Italy:
I will enslave them, just as I will take you.

Greece:
See the Italians come out from forty different places.
The Italians are the first to take out their knives,
And attack the Greeks.
Fire, boys, at all of them. Don't let a soul live.
Better to see their blood make the earth red,
Than this terrible Italy to take Greece.

Conclusion:
The Greek evzones made three attacks.
Many Italians, from their fear and bitter terror,
Threw away their guns,
While others ran away quickly.
Still others dove into the rivers,
And others surrendered into the hands of the Greeks.

EUROPE*

Hit, Europe! They put the cross as a mark on you.
Up high, their half moon hand makes a mosque out of each tall bell tower,
So that a Christian never finds any place for worship.
The altar he has in his heart suffices.
Hit, Europe! Your bombs fly to the borders.
Hit, to see the glitter on Souli once more.
Mount Pindos and Mount Olympus greet you with blood,
And Regas is revived at the waters of Istrous.
Hit, and from your bombs the laurel will take root,
Dense and red in the coolness of March.
You will see our great Greece crowned,
And she will be illuminated with the golden lights of the cross.

HITLER AND VICTORY*

Hitler, you lost the victory!
You took from Greece
The unsleeping torch
To burn London.
Instead, you burned Berlin!

TO MY COUNTRY*

Every night, as I sleep I see you, my country,
Beautiful, blue and white, beloved country.
In the sweetest dream I embrace you!
My friends, male and female!
I can never forget them.
I can't, my country, live in foreign lands.
Exile has poisons that can poison me.
I wish I were a bird that could fly,
To fly back to you, my country, to see you,
To embrace you again.
I will come to see my friends
To kiss them all,
To see your sweetness,
Your glorious places
With a word of respect I respond to you my beloved country.
I never forget you, I will never forget you.
I have an obligation, my country, to understand,
In order, with respect, to teach your language,
Your glory, and all your worthiness of respect.
I walk in foreign lands, like a solitary bird
Without leaves in the straits, without dancing or feasts,
But only work, food, shame, and pain.
Exile has only that, and nothing else.
I am burdened by exile, I am burdened by foreign lands.
To you, my beloved country, I want to return.

HYMN OF LOVE*

A better word
Does not exist
To have in its tone
Such a harmony.
To have in its tone
Such a harmony,
So as to harmonize
With the community.
In this burning heat,
Where we are in the foreign lands,
Brothers, let us first
Be loving to each other.
And when with love
Our heart is decorated,
Then we will live
Happily forever.
Only with love
And with solidarity
Will we win
Super happiness.
Love brings
To the community
Joy and happiness,
Feasting and life.
When time
Despises us,
Then our love
Will despise it.
O, you brothers
Who are beloved,
Let us embrace
And kiss.
As the poet Fereos said,
Brothers do not forget,
Ever in their lives,

This sweet brotherly love.
Only by these words,
Come so we may embrace
And kiss
With that warm, brotherly kiss.

GLORY

Glory to the spirit of the Ancient
World's fountain.
Glory to the guns of hero youths,
Who glorified this earth.
For their great experience
And holy passion
Make new history,
Full of glory and honor.
The victory still brings crowns
To the community tree.
Unstepped on, glorious streets
Await the hero.
Let's go! To our work of games!
There is the Pyrian Palm.
There is the victorious crown,
And the immortal kiss.

WHAT WILL HAPPEN IF THERE IS A THIRD WORLD WAR?

Unconquerable, indomitable, and brave.
If there is a World War III, so what?
Our Lord will scatter
His rich charity, and in our hearts
There will be joy.
Fiery, large swords will break up the storms.
Our guns will again make history with death,
And encourage heroes and
Freedom-lovers.

As the Babylonians and Persians were broken,
Fire will spread acre to acre,
And we will be brave forever,
Without troubled hearts.
Our enemy will be broken,
With fire everywhere.
We, the brave, shall go to war
For Democracy.
We know that the storm will pass!
World War III, if it comes,
Can only harm the body,
Not our beliefs, nor our soul.
Those are truly ours to keep.
We live in the heavenly light.
It's enough for us to be together,
As brothers, side by side.
We shall bravely say
What Pericles said
At the battle of Thermopylae,
"Liberty or Death!"
The hurts and losses will pass,
And blow away forever.
Then, snowy doves and nightingales will sing
OUR INDEPENDENCE HYMN.
Indomitable, unconquerable, and brave.
What will happen if there is a Third World War?
In your believing light,
You, Lord, will be victorious.

KOREA

IN KOREA*

November 2, 1950

In Korea of Asia,
The Reds were celebrating
Because they were able
To conquer half of the south.

But, finally, the time came
For the Democratics
To make the poor Reds
Run like rabbits.

Their leader, Stalin,
Is looking from a high tower.
The Korean Reds are running double time
To meet him in Moscow.

HONOR

We leave our homes
To tell our people good-bye,
And we are going to guard
Our country's honor.

We are all brothers
And soldiers of the U.S.
We shall fight the battle
For our country's honor.

The enemy bullets
We shall never fear
Because we are people,
People of God.

We are all brothers
And soldiers of the U.S.
We shall fight for faith
And freedom to God.

EVENING PRAYER

I pray to thee O Lord, Jesus Christ, Our King.
As the day has come to an end, and the darkness has come,
Again, my fear grows bitter, my heart totters, my body
Weathers, in this open fearful place in Korea.

I beseech thee O Lord to give me a powerful mind
To think best, and to give me the power to sleep free,
Safely, and unthinkingly this night.

Give grace O Lord to my parents, brothers,
Friends, even to our enemy. Make them understand
The freedom and good will of all people, that we ask for.
Give rest to those dying in the battlefield,
And therapy to the wounded, and courage
To all other battling brothers, to overcome and return
Safe back home, to our homes and our loved ones.

I thank Thee O Lord for protecting me and
My parents and all my friends, now and ever more. Amen.

Don't you cry your tears for me,
I shall return.

MY FOXHOLE

On a high, high mount,
In Korea, wild lads,
We stopped for a night
Under enemy fire.

And I took my tranching tool
To build my foxhole
Under enemy fire.

So you can see,
The enemy bullets
Couldn't hit me
In my foxhole,
Which was painted with mud
The color black.

It was a muddy,
A bloody, night
About which I can
Hardly explain the details.

There were many
Of our heroes
Wounded in action,
And on hand to call me
For treatment:
Doc, there,
Doc, here,
Medic, there,
And medic, here.

The voices were
Coming to my ears.

It was a muddy,

A bloody, night
For memories
Of centuries.

And, poor me,
I built my foxhole,
But had no time to sleep in it.

EASTER IN KOREA

Easter today, Easter,
Everywhere is joy,
But we in Korea
Are fighting the war.

O, can't you see
That we are to be free
And live together
At "home sweet home."

But the day is mad,
Raining and snowing both,
And my hands in blood
Tying heroes' wounds.

This Easter in Korea
Is a test by our Lord,
Seeing and believing
That he will save us.

NO!

Let us now
Enter the game
With interest
And faith to freedom.

Let us now
Listen clearly
To our Country
Calling us.

Let us now get the rifle
And enter the battle
To fight for our freedom
And honor,

As the Hero Hellenic Evzones
In World War II
Answered "No" to Mussolini,
Who wanted to enslave
Their Country.

And we have
Done the same.
We told Joe,
NO, NO, NO.

Joe Stalin,
Where are you going?
It's enough now.
Stop here.

Let us now, U.N. men,
Enter the game of heroism
To defend against
The gremlin tyrants,

If you do want
To have your freedom,
Your life, your heritage,
And honorable bread.

COMPANY "B"

John wrote: "I am a medical combat technician attached to 'Baker' Company, Ninth Infantry Regiment of the Second Division in Korea. Since I came to this Company, we met a few battles where the victory was ours. I have the feeling of courage to mention that 'Baker' Company is one of the best outfits in the Regiment."

On the mountains of Korea
I hear the heavy groan,
While the days slowly pass,
And the sun gets dark.

I see there in that village
Our shining bayonets
And the rifle singing
Like nightfall, day and night.

And our heavy mortars
Fall like thunder
On the bodies
Of the enemy.

There are the glorious heroes
Who in freedom learned to live.
There are the hero men
Of the Company "B."

I SHALL RETURN

John wrote: "I picked this poem from a letter I sent to my mother on March 6, 1951 from Korea."

Don't cry
Sweet mother,
Don't you cry your tears,
Don't you worry for me,
I shall return.

Back to our sweet home
I shall come to live,
To your sweet lap, Mama.
Don't worry, and do not cry,
I shall return.

O, you almighty God,
Where you direct
The world from above,
Give powers to all men
Now fighting in Korea

To return to their home.
Make all Nations realize
They must be brothers
And live with peace
Everywhere.

My daily prayers
Are lifted high
To our Lord, Jesus Christ,
To look upon all people
Everywhere.

His powers, Mama,
Shall act
And shall be done

As he wants to be done
Everywhere.

O, Mama, sweet mama,
Don't worry, I shall
Come back to you.
Don't you cry your tears for me,
I shall return.

LOVE

MY ADVICE*

Imagine, girl,
How you will grow old,
And lose your youth
In a short time.
You will cry, you'll be sad,
And you'll be silent,
When you quickly reach
Thirty years old.
When you are forty,
You will leave behind ornaments
Because your hair will turn white,
And you will wear glasses.
When you are fifty,
Your face will wrinkle
And your body will become wounded,
Then you won't be able to bear anymore.
When you become deaf,
You'll be worth nothing.
You will sit on your chair
And stay there forever.
You will be closed up in your house,
Leaning on the walls.
You will be forced to walk on the earth
With your walking stick.

Your teeth will fall out.
At sixty years old,
You will totter,
And you will be deaf.
The doctor will always
Be writing prescriptions.
And then soon, at night,
You will be able to eat nothing.
In front of young ladies,
You will be a curious sight.
You will be sorry
As they laugh at you.
All this, young lady,
You will regret
If you do not love
With the passion of your soul.
Because you will grow old,
And lose your youth.
Then you will want to love,
But you will not be able.

FALSE OATH*

One winter night,
When we were together,
We disregarded the cold
And we talked sweetly.
Don't you remember how many words,
With your treacherous lips,
Sweet, former friend,
You spoke about love?
You forgot everything:
Oath, belief, and friendship.
In your hard heart,
No feeling lives.
Where is that era
Of love and sweetness
That was the source
Of our first happiness and desire?
Based on your false oath,
Who was deluded,
Thinking you loved him,
So that he fell in love with you?

TO THE YOUNG LADY*

Little, sweet bird,
Before you stretch your wings,
Look right, look left,
So you don't go astray.
You have many dangers to be scared of
Before you have learned
How to fly in the skies,
So be careful of misfortune.
You will see below you
The green branches

With cool leaves,
And full of flowers.
A small animal may be hidden,
Covered with those flowers.
So, woe to the bird
That carelessly goes out.
Here, in this little stream,
Cold water is running
With joy,
A breeze cools your chest.
Don't try to fly carelessly,
Little bird that I love.
Don't forget that the little breeze
Becomes a strong North wind.
Be careful, always, be careful
Before you stretch your wings.
Look right, look left,
So you don't go astray.
The hunter may catch
A bird that flies carelessly,
Or the eagle may grab it
In his terrible talons.

SWEET FRIEND*

Harsh one, remember how you told me,
How you told me that you love me.
Now, you act like you don't see me,
And when you see me, you laugh!
You were not harsh before.
Oh, how you changed.
Sweet friend, how you forgot me.
You now say sweet words to another.
To another, you say, "You are my lover,
My lover forever."
You never think of me, however,
Like last year's news.

What was it like last year?
It was a time of love, a time of sweetness,
And much happier even
Than my childhood.
Time passes easily, my friend,
But love stays forever.
It stays in the person,
Bringing death painlessly and soon.

REMEMBER*

Remember our love, unmerciful one,
Our sweet pains, our sorrows.
Remember, unmoved one, our tears,
So many of our hurts, and our complaints.
Remember, unfeeling one, how you thought of me
When you placed me on a pedestal,
Where you kissed me softly, trembling,
And I answered with groans?
First, you appeared before me,
And I saw your angelic beauty.
As a beautiful picture, I shut you in my heart.
I became part of you with one glance.
Oh! Yes, I loved you, and I had hope
To live with you forever.
But when I opened your heart,
I saw a betrayer.
Yes, I loved you! Unhappy time,
Unhappy and dark day,
Why do you send me now to my grave
With one bitter, deep wound?

THE FIRST TIME I SAW YOU*

The first time I saw you,
Why did you open my heart?
Why did you encourage me,
If you did not want to stay true?
Like a fire that is beginning to go out,
Leaving only ashes,
That's the way love will stay with me
Until my innocent soul goes out.
Then, hard one, you will cry
When you see how I die for you,
When you see cotton
On my lips.
Lonely, you'll come to my grave.
You will make my grave beautiful with flowers.
You will spill groaning tears
Over the body that is enclosed there.
You will be dressed in black.
You'll always remember me, and you'll cry for me forever.
A golden day will come
When you will place myrtle on my grave.
Myrtle, roses, and flowers of paradise.
Always, with tears, you will want me.
Those sweet eyes
That bring a horrible, burning heat to the heart.

LOVE

I want to leave this people.
I want to leave the mountain,
With the flowers of earth,
To die fighting the lion.
And yet, I can't ever leave it,
And go far away
From that tree where I was lying,
And where I loved for so long,
I have a fire in my chest
That burns me, making me so old, so hard.
In my heart, no blood remains,
Because love has burned my heart.
I cry, groan,
And wail inconsolably.
After love ends,
How wretched I am.

THE LAMENTATION

The heat of the sun is frozen.
Like fire, my chest burns.
No fountain has so much water flowing,
As the tears that I spill, my miserable self.
My heart starts to groan
With the force of the winds.
Death's knife does not cut
Like you, with your hard eyes.
You, clear moon, where do you go,
And how do you know all my misfortunes?
If you see that pitiless woman, tell her
That she opens my grave with her hardness.
Run, run, before my soul
Leaves my miserable body.
Run, run, the heavens are opening.
Run, run, the clouds in the sky are now flying.

POEMS IN GREEK

ΦΙΛΟΣΟΦΙΑ

Εἶδα τόν διδάσκαλον ἀπό αὐτούς πού ξεύρω
ἐν μέσῳ τῆς φιλοσοφικῆς οἰκογενείας
ἀπό ὅλην τήν γῆν θαυμασμόν καί εὐλαβείας
τόν Πλάτωνα ἔχω εἰδῆ καί τόν Σωκράτη
οἱ ὁποῖοι στέκουν πρῶτοι αὐτοί καί μετά δέ καί οἱ ὑπόλοιποι.

ΤΟΥ ΘΕΟΥ Η ΕΥΛΟΓΙΑ

Σκόρπισε τήν εὐλογίαν σου
ὄχι μόνο εἰς τήν χώραν μας αὐτήν
ἀλλ' ἀπ' ἄκρον εἰς ἄκρον τοῦ κόσμου
κάμε ὦ Θεέ τά ἔθνη νά ἰδοῦν
ὅτι οἱ ἄνθρωποι ἀδέλφια νά εἶναι
καί οἰκογένειαν μία ν' ἀποτελοῦν.

Ο ΘΕΟΣ

Θέε ὑμνεῖ τήν δόξα σου ἡ νύξ καί ἡ μέρα
μέ ἄνθη ἔστρωσες τήν γῆν, μέ ἄστρα τόν αἰθέρα
τῆς γῆς ἀσύμφων' οἱ λαοί αἰνοῦσί σε συγχρόνως
ποικίλαι γλῶσσαι χείλια ὑμνοῦσι σε συμφώνως,
τό πᾶν ἀμέτρητο μετρᾷς, ἀόριστο ὁρίζεις
τό πᾶν ἀόρατο ὁρᾷς, ἀγνώριστο γνωρίζεις.

Τό φῶς, Θέε τό σῶμα σου,
ὁ ἥλιος τό ὄμμα σου,
ὁ κεραυνός φωνή σου.

Τό ἄπειρον διάστημα
τό μέγα σου ἀνάστημα,
καί ὁ αἰών στιγμή σου.

Δύναται ὁ δάκτυλός σου
ὡς μοχλός τήν γῆν νά σείση.

Καί τό κοῖλον τῆς χειρός σου
τούς ὠκεανούς νά κλείση.

Ἐν σοί πνεῦμα μόνον σβύνει
τῶν ἀστέρων τούς φανούς.

Ἐν σοί νεῦμα μόνον κλίνει
πρός τήν γῆν τούς οὐρανούς.

ΠΟΛΕΜΙΣΤΗΡΙΟΝ

Στήν παλάμη καί πάλιν τό σπαθί, τό σπαθί,
καί τό αἷμα ποτάμι, καί τό αἷμα ἄς χυθῆ
μᾶς φωνάζουν πρῶτοι οἱ Ἰταλοί καί μετά οἱ Γερμανοί.
Νά Θεσσαλοί, Ἠπειρῶται, Μακεδόνες καί Θράκες
Ὁ Ἄθως εἰς αἷμα, καί ἡ Πίνδος ἡ Ὄσσα
μεταφέρουν ἐκείνων τήν βροντόφωνη γλῶσσα,
ἀντί σίτου πυρῖτις εἰς τήν γῆν σπαρμένη,
ἕναν μόνον σπινθήρα, ἕνα μόνον προσμένει,
τῆς Ἑλλάδος οἱ παῖδες, σεῖς γενῆτε σπινθῆρες,
Στρατηγοί των γενῆτε καί τοῦ γένους φωστῆρες.

ΤΟ ΚΑΡΠΕΝΗΣΙ

Ματωμένη ὡς τήν ὑστέρην ὥρα
καί ἀπ' τίς φλόγες ἀκόμα ζεστή
ἡ τρισένδοξος γῆ δαφνοφόρα
τά δεσμά τῆς Λειβαδιᾶς πατεῖ.

Χαῖρε ὦ Καρπενήσιον Αἱμάτων αἰῶνες
στήν γλυκεῖα σου σκιρτοῦν 'λευθεριά
τάφοι δόξας κι ὑπέρλαμπροι ἀγῶνες
τή λαμπρή σου στολίζουν θωριά.

Μέ ἅγια δάκρυα τό δρόμον σου σπέρνεις
τῆς μητρός σου ὁ παλμός ὁ κρυφός,
κ' ἕνα σπλάγχνο τόν θρόνον της στρώνεις
ἀρραβῶνα στό οὐράνιο σου φῶς

ΩΔΗ ΠΡΟΣ ΤΟΥΣ ΕΛΛΗΝΑΣ

Ἄγριος τίγρις, δεινόν θηρίον
Ἰταλῶν Μουσουλίνη, εὐνούχου θρέμμα,
ρουφᾶ μέ λύσσα ἑλληνικόν αἷμα,
αἷμα γερόντων, ἀνδρῶν, καί νηπίων

Προστάζουν φόνον ἑλλήνων ἡρώων,
ὁπλιτῶν πλῆθος πανταχοῦ στέλει
ἀλλ' ὁ στρατός του, δούλου ἀγέλη,
ὁ δέ Στρατός μας, Στρατός ἡρώων.

Μά τήν ἀντέττε χειρῶν βίαν,
τάφρους, ἐπάλξεις, ὕψη φρουρίων,
καί πῦρ ἀπείρων τῶν κανονίων
πρό τῶν Ἑλλήνων τήν εὐψυχίαν.

Κατά τῆς νέας ἤδη Περσίας
νέοι ἀγῶνες εἰς Θερμοπύλας,
τῆς παμποθήτου Ἀθανασίας.

ΠΟΛΕΜΙΣΤΗΡΙΟΝ

Λυποῦμαι πού ἐσκόρπιζεν ἡ ἄσωτος καρδιά μου
ἐδῶ κ' ἐκεῖ παροδικά τόσα αἰσθήματά μου,
καί δέν τά' φύλαγε ἡ φτωχή πού νά τό ἔχῃ τώρα,
στό ζηλεμένο μου χωριό νά τά προσφέρῃ δῶρα·
Ὅση κι ἄν μοῦ' μενε δροσιά εἰς τήν καρδιά ἀκόμα
δάκρυα χάρος τά πότησα στ' ἀθάνατό σας χῶμα.
Ἐδῶ πού' θᾶχα αἰώνια ἡ δόξα ἡ πανήγυρις,
γιά νά στολίζω μέ ἔλατα, καί δάφνα τό Βελοῦχι.

Ἄχ νά τό στόλιζα καί ἐγώ μ' ἕνα φτωχό λουλούδι,
κι ἄς ἤτανε τῆς λύρας μου τό ὑστερνό τραγοῦδι,
τόσο πολύ σᾶς ἀγαπῶ, γιατί δέν τό γνωρίζω.
Ὅρκο σᾶς κάνω στό Θεό, στά ξένα πού γυρίζω.
Ἄν πέρασα μιά στιγμή, δέν θά περάσῃ ὥρα,
νά μή θυμοῦμαϊ τῶν Καρπενησίων, τή ζηλεμένη χώρα
γιά τοῦτο σᾶς παρακαλῶ νά μή μοῦ λησμονᾶτε,
ὅποιος στόν κόσμο ἀγαπᾶ πρέπει καί ν' ἀγαπᾶται
κι ἐκείνη ἡ ἐνθύμιση τόν πόνο θά' λαφρώνῃ,
νά κελαϊδῇ χαρούμενο καμμιά φορά τ' ἀηδόνι
μέσα στήν μαύρη του σκλαβιά στήν ἔρημη Βελουχία
ἀφοῦ ἡ μοῖρα τοῦ' γραψε τέτοια λογῆς κατάρα.

Ἀνάθεμά σε, ξενιτειά, πού μοῦ' φαγες τά νειᾶτα
καί δέν μ' ἀφήνεις νά χαρῶ
τά παλικάρια πού θορῶ
πού' ναι γεμάτα λεβεντιά
πού' ναι καρδιά γεμάτα.
Μισεύω, Καρπενήσι μου γλυκό, μέ πόνο σέ ἀφήνω
πάγω στή μαύρη μου σκλαβιά,
μά τή πτωχή μου τήν καρδιά
σέ σένα τήν ἀφήνω.
Ἔχετ' γειά, σταυραετοί, ἔχε' γειά, χωριό μου
Κι ἐμένα λησμονήσατε, ἀλλ' ὄχι τήν καρδιά μου.

ΤΡΟΜΑΡΑ ΤΩΝ ΙΤΑΛΩΝ ΣΤΗΝ ΑΛΒΑΝΙΑ

Σταθῆτ' ἐδῶ, βρέ Ἰταλοί, σταθῆτε νά μοῦ πῆτε,
κοντά σ' ἐμέ τί θέλετε, πού τόπος σας δέν εἶμαι;
Ἐγώ 'μαι χώρα Ἑλληνικιά, καί σκλάβα δέν θά ζήσω
Πατρίδα τ' Ἀλεξάνδρου μου καί τοῦ Ἀριστοτέλη
π' ὅλον τόν κόσμο φώτησαν κι' ἀκόμα τόν φωτίζουν.

Ἐμεῖς θέ' νά σοῦ πάρουμε τήν τόση ὀμορφιά σου
ἔχεις μέρη ζηλευτά, ἔχεις βουνά σάν κάστρα,
ἔχεις ραχοῦλες καί νερά, ἔχεις πολλά καπήκια,
καί σκλάβα μας θά σ' ἔχουμε δουλεύτρα στά παιδιά μας

Σκλάβα σ' ἐσᾶς δέν γίνομαι κακή τατάρων γένα
μέσα μου βράζ' ἀδιάκοπα τῆς Μάνας μου τό αἷμα,
κι ἄν τύχη λίγο καί χυθῇ, τήν γῆν καί κοκινήσῃ,
θά δῇς νά βγάλ' αὐτή ἡ γῆ φωτιές πού θά σᾶς κάψουν.
Ἔγινα σκλάβα μιά φορά γιατ' ἤτανε γραφτό μου.

Ὁ Τοῦρκος μ' ἐσεβάστηκε μ' ἔσωσα τήν τιμή μου
ἔσωσα καί τήν πίστη μου καί τή ζωή μ' ἀκόμα
κι' ἄν θέλῃ ὁ Θεός μέ νίκη πλειά θά ζῶ εὐτυχισμένη
σεῖς χωρισθήκατ' ἀπό μέ κ' ἀφορισμένοι εἶσθε,
τραβᾶτε πέρα Ἰταλοί κυτᾶτε τή δουλειά σας.

Ἔλα χρυσή κοπέλα μας, γίνε καί σύ Ἰταλίδα
ἔλα νά πάρῃς Ἰταλό, ὅπου φορεῖ καλπάκι
γιατί εἰς αὐτοῦ παντέρημη καί σκοτεινή καί μαύρη
καί κοντινό σου συγγενή κανένανε δέν ἔχεις
κανένα ἐμπιστευτικό, μηδέ μαντατοφόρο,
νά τρέξῃ καί τόν πόνο σου νά πάῃ νά φανερώσῃ.

Τό ξέρτε δέν παντρεύομαι, ἐλεύθερη θά ζήσω
παρά νά πάρω Ἰταλό, στή μάνα μου θά πάω
Ἑλλαδικούς μου μή θαρρῇς, δέν ἔχω τάχα κι ἄλλους
ἔχω τήν Ρούμελη ἀδερφή, καί τόν Μωριά ἀδέρφι,
καί τά νησιά' δερφάκια μου, τήν Κρήτη ἀδερφούλα
κι ἀλοίμονό σας ἄν κάνουν κατ' ἐδῶ.

Αὐτούς θά τούς σκλαβώσωμε σάν πάρωμε ἐσένα.

Τόν λόγον δέν ἀπόσωσαν τόν λόγον δέν ἀποεῖπαν
Ποῦ 'στε Ἰταλιάνοι, τώρα π' ὁλοῦθε μέ φυλᾶτε;
καί νά οἱ Ἰταλιάνοι πρόβαλαν ἀπό σαράντα μέρη
πρῶτοι τραβᾶνε τά σπαθιά καί πρῶτοι τούς φωνάζουν

Φωτιά, παιδιά, σέ ὅλους τους ψυχή μήν ἀπομείνη,
κάλλιο νά ἰδοῦν τό αἷμα τους τή γῆ νά καταβάψη,
παρά αὐτή τή βλάμισα 'Ιταλία νά τήν πάρη.

Τρία γιορούσια κάνουνε ἡ Ἕλληνες Τσολιάδες
κι 'Ιταλοί ἀπ' τό φόβο τους κι τήν πικρή τρομάρα τους
ἄλλοι πετοῦνε τ' ἄρματα, ἄλλοι πιλάλα φεύγουν,
ἄλλοι ἀπ' τήν τρομάρα τους μέσ' τά ποτάμια πέφτουν,
καί ἄλλοι παραδίνονται στά χέρια τῶν Ἑλλήνων.

ΕΥΡΩΠΗ

Κτύπα Εὐρώπη Σοῦ' βαλαν σημάδι τό σταυρό
ψηλά τό μισοφέγγαρο τό χέρι σου νά στήση
κάνε τζαμί τό κάθε της ψηλό καμπαναριό
τόπο μή βρῇ ὁ χριστιανός ποτέ νά προσκυνήση
τόν φθάνει μόνον ὁ βωμός πού ἔχει στήν καρδιά,
σέ μιά εἰκόνα, δύο θεές λατρεύει μέ καμάρι
κ' οἱ δύο μαζί φτερώνουνε τῆς Κρήτης τά παιδιά
βαθύτερον ν' ἀνοίξουνε τό μνῆμα στό φεγγάρι

Κτύπα, Εὐρώπη οἱ βόμβες σου στά σύνορα πετοῦν
κτύπα νά δῆς ἀναλαμπές στό Σούλι μιά φορά
Ἡ Πίνδος καί ὁ Ὄλυμπος τόν Αἶμο χαιρετοῦνε
κι ὁ Ρήγας ἀνασταίνεται στοῦ Ἴστρου τά νερά.

Κτύπα κι ἀπό τίς βόμβες σου ἡ δάφνη θά φυτρώση
πιό φουντωτή πιό κόκκινη στοῦ Μάρτη τή δροσιά
μεγάλη τήν Ἑλλάδα μας θά δῆς νά στεφανώση
καί τοῦ σταυροῦ θά λάμψουνε τά φῶτα τά χρυσά.

ΧΙΤΛΕΡ ΚΑΙ ΝΙΚΗ

Χίτλερ Ὀλυμπιανίκη
πάλι ἔχασες τή νίκη
πῆρες ἀπό τήν Ἑλλάδα
τήν ἀκοίμητη λαμπάδα
γιά νά κάψης τό Λονδίνο
κι ἔκαψες τό Βερολίνο.

ΣΤΗΝ ΠΑΤΡΙΔΑ ΜΟΥ

Κάθε βραδιά στόν ὕπνο μου πατρίδα μου σε βλέπω
ὡραία γαλανόλευκη πατρίδα ἠγαπημένη.

Σέ ὄνειρο γλυκύτατο ἐσένα ἀγκαλιάζω
τούς φίλους μου τίς φίλες μου
δέ μπορῶ ποτές μου νά ξεχάσω.

Δέν μπορῶ πατρίδα μου στά ξένα γιά νά ζήσω
ἡ ξενιτειά ἔχει φάρμακα καί θά μέ φαρμακώση.

Εἴθελα νάμουνα πουλάκι φτερωτό
πατρίς μου νά πετάξω πάλι νά σέ δῶ
πάλι νά σέ ἀγκαλιάσω.

Νά᾿ λθω νά δῶ τούς φίλους μου
τίς φίλες μου ὅλους νά τούς φιλήσω,
νά δῶ ὅλες τίς γλύκες σου
τά δοξασμένα μέρη.

Λόγον τιμῆς σοῦ ἀπαντῶ πατρίς μου ἀγαπημένη,
ἐγώ ποτέ δέν σέ ξεχνῶ ποτές δέν σέ ξεχνάω

Καί ἔχω ὑποχρέωση, πατρίδα μου τό νιώθω,
γιά νά διδάξω μέ τιμή, τή γλῶσσα σου,
τή δόξα σου, καί ὅλη τήν τιμιότητά σου.

Μέσα στά ξένα περπατῶ, σάν ἔρημο πουλάκι
χωρίς φιλιά μές τά στενά, χωρίς χορό καί γλέντι,
παρά μονάχα στή δουλειά φαΐ, ποτί καί ὕπνο.
Αὐτό ἔχει ἡ ξενιτειά μονάχα καί τίποτ᾿ ἄλλο.

Βαρέθηκα τήν ξενιτειά, βαρέθηκα τά ξένα,
σέ σένα ἀγαπημένη μου πατρίς ποθῶ γιά νά γυρίσω.

ΥΜΝΟΣ ΤΗΣ ΑΓΑΠΗΣ

Καλύτερη λέξη
δέν βρίσκεται ἄλλη καμία
νά' χη στόν ἦχο της
τέτοια ἁρμονία.

Νά' χη στό ἦχο της
τέτοια ἁρμονία
ὥστε νά ἁρμόζη
εἰς τήν κοινωνία.

Μές σέ τούτη λαύρα
πού' μαστε στά ξένα,
πρώτη ἐμεῖς τά ἀδέρφια
νά' μαστε ἀγαπημένα.

Καί ὅταν μέ ἀγάπη
στολίζετε ἡ καρδιά μας
τότε θέ νά ζῶμε
εὐτυχεῖς γιά πάντα.

Μόνο μέ ἀγάπη
καί μέ ἀλληλεγγύη
θέ γιά νά κερδίσωμε
τά ὑπέρ εὐτυχίας.

Ἡ ἀγάπη φέρνει
εἰς τήν κοινωνία
χαρά καί εὐτυχία
γλέντι καί ζωή.

Ὅταν κάποια ὥρα
μᾶς περιφρονεῖ
τότε ἡ ἀγάπη μας
τήν καταφρονεῖ.

Ὦ Ἐσεῖς ἀδέρφια
πού ἀγαπημένα
ἄς ἀγκαλιαστοῦμε
γιά νά ἀσπαστοῦμε.

"Οπως ἔχει πεῖ
ποιητής Φεραῖος, τά ἀδέρφια δέν ξεχνοῦνε
ποτέ τους στή ζωή
γιά τή αὐτή ἡ γλυκειά ἀγάπη ἀδελφική.

Μ' αὐτά μόνον τά λόγια
ἐλάτε νά ἀγκαλιαστοῦμε
γιά νά ἀσπαστοῦμε
τό θερμό ἐκεῖνο ἀδελφικό φιλί.

ΣΤΗΝ ΚΟΡΕΑ

Εἰς τήν Κορέα τῆς Ἀσίας
οἱ ἐχθροί χορεύουν
γιατί ἐκατόρθωσαν
νά μισοκατακτήσουν τήν Νότιο Κορέα.
Γιατί οἱ δημοκρατικοί
δέν εἴχανε ἰδέα.

Μά τώρα ἦλθε ἡ στιγμή
πού οἱ δημοκρατικοί
ἐκάνανε τούς ἐχθρούς
νά τρέχουν σάν λαγούς.

Κι' ὁ Στάλιν ἀπό ψηλά
κυττάει τούς κόκκινους
πού πάνε κατ' εὐθείαν
τρέχοντας νά ἀνταμώσουν
στήν Μόσχοβο.

ΣΥΜΒΟΥΛΗ

Στοχάσου κοπέλα,
πώς θέ νά γεράσης
τή νειοτή θά χάσης
σ' ὀλίγον καιρό

Θά κλαῖς, θά λυπᾶσαι,
καί θά κρυφοσκάσης
εὐθύς μόλις φθάσης
τριάντα χρονῶν.

Σάν πᾶς στούς σαράντα
στολίδια θά' φήσης
γιατί θέ νά' σπρίσης
θά βάλης γυαλιά

Πενῆντα σάν φθάσης
τά μοῦτρα ζαρόνουν
τά μέλη πληγώνουν
καί πλειά δέν μπορεῖς.

Ἔ τότε κουφίζεις,
σολδί δέν ἀξίζεις
στό σκαμνίο σου πρέπει
νά γνέθης σκουλιά.

Στό σπίτι θά κλείεσαι
στούς τοίχους θά στιέσαι
καί μέ τό μπαστοῦνι
στή γῆ θά πατῆς

Τά δόντια σάν πέσουν
στά ἑξῆντα, τρικλίζεις
κακά θά κουφίζης
καί πάντα ὁ γιατρός.

Θά γράφη ρετσέτες
νά βάνης πετσέτες
γιά γιόμα καί βράδυ
πανάδα θά τρῶς.

Ἐμπρός εἰς τίς νέες
περίγελο θά' σαι
ἐσύ θά λυπᾶσαι
κ' ἐκεῖνες θά γελοῦν.

Διά τοῦτο κυρά μου
θά μετανοήσης
ἄν δέν ἀγαπήσης
μέ πάθος ψυχῆς.

Γιατί θά γεράσης
τή νειοτή θά χάσης
καί τότε θά θέλης
μά δέν θά μπορῆς.

ΕΠΙΟΡΚΙΑ

Ἕνα βράδυ τόν χειμῶνα
ὅταν ἤμεθα οἱ δύο
κι ἀψηφούσαμε τό κρύο
κι ὁμιλούσαμε γλυκά.

Δέν θυμᾶσαι πόσα λόγια
μέ τά δόλιά σου χείλη,
ὦ γλυκεῖα τότε φίλη,
μ' ἔλεγες ἐρωτικά;

Ἐλησμόνησες τά πάντα
ὅρκους, πίστι καί φιλιά
στήν σκληράν σου τήν καρδία
κανέν αἴσθημα δέν ζεῖ.

Ποῦ ἡ ἐποχή ἐκείνη
τῶν ἐρώτων ἡ γλυκεῖα
ποῦ ἡ πρώτη εὐτυχία
καί τῶν πόθων ἡ πηγή

Στούς ψευδούς σου τώρα ὅρκους
ποῖος τάχα νά πλανᾶται
καί φρονεῖ πώς ἀγαπᾶται
καί ὁ μωρός σέ ἀγαπᾶ;

Πλήν θά μάθης ὅτι ἔχει
μίαν χάριν τήν ψυχήν σου
τόν ἀθῶον ἐραστήν σου
αἰωνίως ν' ἀπαντᾶ.

ΕΙΣ ΝΕΑΝΙΔΑ

Πουλάκι μικροφτέρουγο,
πρίν τά φτερά τα' νοίξεις
κύττα δεξιά κύττα ζερβά
νά μή παραστρατήσης.

Έχεις πολλούς νά φοβηθῆς
κινδύνους πρῶτον νά μάθης
εἰς τούς αἰθέρας πού πετᾶς
καί πρόσεξε μήν πάθης.

Σ' αὐτά πού βλέπεις τά κλαδιά
τά πράσινα κεῖ κάτου,
ὅπου μέ φύλλα δροσερά
κι' ἄνθους εἶναι γεμάτο.

Παγίδα ἴσως κρύπτεται
μέ ἄνθη σκεπασμένη,
κι' ἀλλοίμονον εἰς τό πουλί
π' ἀπρόσεκτα διαβαίνει.

Ἐδῶ σ' αὐτή τή ρεματιά
πού τρέχει κρύο νεράκι,
πού σοῦ δροσίζει μέ χαρά
τά στήθη κ' ἀεράκι.

Μή ξέχνιαστα τό πέταμα
πουλάκι σταματήσης,
καί πῶς ἡ αὔρα γίνεται
βοριᾶς μή λησμονήσης.

Πρόσεχε πάντα πρόσεχε
πρίν τά φτερά τα' νοίξεις
κύττα δεξιά κύττα ζερβά
νά μή παραστρατήσης.

Πουλί π' ἀπρόσεκτα πετᾶ
ὁ κυνηγός τό πιάνει
ὁ ἀετός στά νύχια του
τά φοβερά τό βάνει.

ΓΛΥΚΕΙΑ ΦΙΛΗ

Σκληρά θυμᾶσαι ποσάκις μ' εἶπες
ποσάκις μ' εἶπες πῶς μ' ἀγαπᾶς;
καί τώρα κάμνεις πῶς δέν μέ εἶδες
κι ὅταν μέ βλέπεις χομεγελᾶς.

Σκληρά δέν ἦσο, πῶς μεταβλήθης
πῶς μεταβλήθης ἐξαφνικά;
Γλυκεῖα φίλη πῶς μεταβλήθης
κ' εἰς ἄλλον λέγεις λόγια γλυκά;

Εἰς ἄλλον λέγεις ἔρως μου εἶσαι
ἔρως μου εἶσαι παντοτεινός,
κ' ἐμένα πλέον δέν συλλογιέσαι
παρῆλθε ὁ χρόνος ὁ περσινός.

Τί χρόνος ἦτο ὁ περασμένος
χρόνος ἐρώτων, χρόνος γλυκύς
καί πολύ πλέον εὐτυχισμένος
τῆς ἐποχῆς μου τῆς παιδικῆς.

Περνᾶ εὐκόλως, φίλη ὁ χρόνος
ἡ ἀγάπη ὅμως παντοτεινά
μένει στόν ἄνθρωπο καί ἀπόνως
τόν θανατώνει ἐλεεινά.

ΘΥΜΗΣΟΥ

Θυμήσου, ἄσπλαχνη, τόν ἔρωτά μας,
τούς γλυκεῖς πόνους μας, τούς στεναγμούς.
Θυμήσου, ἄπονη, τά δάκρυά μας,
τά τόσα πάθη μας καί τους καϋμούς.

Θυμήσου, ἀναίσθητη, πῶς μ' ἐθεωροῦσες
ὅταν μ' ἀνέβαζες στούς οὐρανούς,
πού γλυκοτρέμοντας μ' ἀγνοφιλοῦσες
κι ἀποκρινόμουνα μέ στεναγμούς.

Πρώτη πού φάνηκες, σκληρά μπροστά μου
κι εἶδα τά κάλλη σου τ' ἀγγελικά
εἰκόνισμα σ' ἔκλεισα μέσ' στήν καρδιά μου
κ' ἔγινα κτῆμα σου μέ μιά ματιά.

Ω ναί σ' αγάπησα κ' είχα ελπίδα
πώς θέ νά ζούσαμε πάντα μαζί
αλλά τά στήθη σου πού άνοιξα κ' είδα,
προδότης δέ μας τά διοικεί.

Άχ ναί, σ' αγάπησα δύστυχη ώρα,
ημέρα άχαρη καί σκοτεινή,
γιατί στό μνήμα μου μέ στέλνεις τώρα
μέ μιά πικρότητα βαθιά πληγή.

ΤΗΝ ΠΡΩΤΗΝ ΦΟΡΑ ΠΟΥ ΣΕ ΕΙΔΑ

Άχ τήν πρώτη φορά πού σέ είδα,
διατί τήν καρδιά μου ν' ανοίξης,
διατί σαΐτες νά ρίψης
σάν δέν ήθελες μείνει πιστή;

Σάν τήν φωτιά πού αρχίζει καί σβύνει
καί τήν τέφρα της πού αφίνει
έτσι ο έρως σ' εμένα θά μείνη
έως νά βγή η αθώα μου ψυχή.

Τότε, τότε, σκηρά θέ νά κλάψης
σάν ίδης πώς γιά σένα πεθαίνω
σάν ίδης τό βαμβάκι βαλμένο
εις τά χείλη μου επάνω τ' ωχρό

Μοναχή εις τόν τάφο μου θά έλθης
καί τήν πλάκα μ' ανθούς θά στολίσης,
καί στενάζουσα δάκρυα θά χύσης
διά τό σώμα πού μέσα της κλεί.

Στά μαύρα ντυμένη, στά μαύρα θέ νά' σαι
καί εμέ θά θυμάσαι καί πάντα θά κλαίς
θά έλθη μιά μέρα χρυσή περιστέρα
στόν τάφο μου' πάνω νά ρίψης μυρτιές.

Μυρτιές καί τριαντάφυλλα, κι άνθη του παραδείσου,
καί πάντα μέ δάκρυα θά λές "ώχ εμέ"
αυτά τά ωραία γλυκύτατα μάτια
μου φέρνουν μάχαιρα φρικτή στήν καρδιά.

ΕΡΩΤΑΣ

Ν' ἀφήσω θέλω τόν κόσμον τοῦτον
νά πάω νά ζήσω σ' ἕνα βουνό
μέ τά λιοντάρια νά τρέφωμαι
μέ τά λιοντάρια νά πολεμῶ.

Αὐτό τό δένδρον κολακεύω
κι ὅπου λατρεύω τόσον καιρόν
δέν θά ἀφήσω ἐγώ ποτέ μου
νά δοκιμάσῃς ἄλλον καρπόν.

Μίαν φλόγα ἔχω μέσα στό στῆθος
ἥτις μέ καίει τόσον δεινῶς,
καί τῆς καρδίας μου δέν ἀφησ' ἴχνος,
μοῦ τήν κατέκαυσεν ὁλοτελῶς.

Κλαίω ὁ ἄθλιος κι ἀναστενάζω
κι ἀπαρηγόρητος θρηνωδῶ,
εἰς, μάτην ὅμως ἔλεος κράζω
"Ἀχ, ὁ καημένος τί θά γίνω

ΘΡΗΝΟΣ

Παγωμένη τοῦ ἡλίου ἡ θερμότης
σάν φωτιά, πού εἰς τά στήθη μου καίει
δέν εἶν βρύσις τόσον ὕδωρ νά ρέη
ὡσάν δάκρυα χύνω ὁ ἄθλιος ἐγώ.

Τῶν ἀνέμων ἡ δύναμις πάνυ
σάν ἀρχιζ' ἡ καρδιά μου νά στενάζῃ
τοῦ θανάτου τό ξίφος δέν σφάζει
σάν ἐσέ τῆς σκληρᾶς μιά ματιά

Σύ σελήνη πού πάντα γυρίζεις
καί τά πάθη μου ὅλα τά ξεύρεις
ἄν δῆς κείνη τήν ἄσπλαγχνη πές της
πῶς τόν τάφο μου ἀνοιγ' ἡ σκληρά.

Τρέξε, τρέξε πρωτοῦ ἡ ψυχή μου
ἀπ' τό ἄθλιον σῶμα μου φύγει,
Τρέξε, τρέξε, αἰθέρα ἀνοίγει
Τρέξε, τρέξε, εἰς τά νέφη πετᾶ.

www.ingramcontent.com/pod-product-compliance
Lightning Source LLC
Chambersburg PA
CBHW031252290426
44109CB00012B/548